A STORY FROM THE BOER WAR

BY
GIDEON LOUW

The characters in this novella are fictitious, but they represent
real people involved in the historical events portrayed.

By the same author:

Louw, G.N.   1993. *Physiological Animal Ecology.*
             Longman, London, U.K.

Louw, G.N.   1996. *Why Elephants and Fleas Don't Sweat.*
             Detselig, Calgary.

ISBN: 0-9730220-1-9

First Published 2002 by: *City Scribe Publishing Co.*
                          1207 Verdier Avenue
                          Brentwood Bay
                          British Columbia
                          Canada

For
   Claire

So tik ek met die handsambok
so ry ek die skimmel handgalop
hy trap die aarde van hom weg
hy maak die ding by die meisie reg
dis baie jare reeds verby
wat het geword van hom en my

Boerneef

Foreword

My Dad's farm was situated on a beautiful, unspoilt tidal river on the east coast of South Africa. Once the farm chores were over there was ample time for boating, fishing, swimming and hiking. We also spent many an evening on our veranda overlooking the river, while enjoying the balmy weather and telling stories to one another. Crickets and tree frogs provided the background music, interrupted quite frequently by splashing mullet rippling the moonlight on the surface of the water. On these occasions Dad would enjoy a good sipping whisky, while he recounted his family's experiences, hardships and successes.

These stories have remained with me for a lifetime and the main reason for writing this novella was to pass some of these on to my children and grandchildren, thereby giving them some understanding of their cultural roots. In addition, the social history of Afrikaner families between 1899 and 1918 has not been well covered through the medium of English. Much of it is biased and it is my hope that this modest contribution might redress this imbalance in a small way.

I wish to thank my family for encouraging me to write this story and particularly my wife, Claire, my daughter Kristin, and Avril Warren who read the manuscript and gave me helpful advice. Sheila Cowan kindly provided the campfire sketch. Peter Belonje and George Spencer advised me on medical and historical facts. Chris Scott contributed valuable editorial suggestions. None of the above is, however, responsible for my many sins of both omission and commission.

Thanks are also due to my publisher, Laurel McIntyre, for her cheerful and enthusiastic guidance.

G.N.L.

Vancouver Island, Canada 2002

1

The road that runs northwest from the South African hamlet of Calvinia winds through a chain of flat-topped hills, or koppies. In the mid-summer of 1899 a British officer was leading a small party of horsemen along this dusty road, while the westering sun turned the buttresses on the koppies to a pale gold. His presence on the road had long since attracted attention and some Boer farmers in the valley were still signalling to one another with home-made heliograph mirrors to report the intrusion.

The officer had orders to wear his full-dress uniform with red tunic and white helmet on these forays into the arid, north-western regions of the Cape Colony; presumably to impress the farmers whose livestock he had come to expropriate for the war. But the heat and dust of the valley had turned his subaltern's uniform into a grimy parody of formality.

Out of the corner of his eye, he was aware of the occasional heliograph signal, flashing in the dying sun and monitoring his progress through the valley. What he did not see was a youngster some 300 yards distant, carefully hidden high above the road by a large rock and the overhanging branches of a waboom. Johan had spread his rough corduroy jacket over the rock to protect the carefully polished stock of a powerful Mauser rifle. Several weeks ago he had paced off the distance between his present hideout and the curve in the road that the British officer was about to reach.

Johan raised the peep sight on the rifle and took careful aim on the officer's torso, waiting for him to reach the target distance. With twenty seconds left, he released the safety catch and curled his finger around the knurled trigger. He could feel the sweat beading on his face as he pressed the stock firmly against his cheek to compensate for the recoil. He kept the scarlet tunic in his sights until the officer moved slowly beyond the range of his rifle.

After a short wait Johan slung his rifle over his shoulder and scrambled down the koppie to a nearby dry gully. Freeing his horse, he mounted in a single fluid movement, talking quietly to it as they picked their way down the rocky scree towards a narrow flood plain, running alongside the dry riverbed. Here he gave the horse its head and dug in his heels, galloping for over a mile before turning back towards the road. He dismounted at the foot of a low koppie, tethered his horse and immediately started to climb.

It took him less than fifteen minutes to reach the top, from where he could follow the progress of the British officer and his party without being detected. Johan saw that the officer was anxious to find a site for his overnight camp. The subaltern had sent his Cape Coloured soldiers to reconnoitre along the dry riverbed that snaked through the valley. Before long they found a suitable place near some wild olive trees and began to prepare their camp.

This was the signal for the youngster to return to his mount and ride hard for his own home, some five miles away. He arrived at the farmyard at dusk but before stabling his horse, he led it quietly around to cool while his mind raced with the import of what he had just seen. More than once he heard his mother calling anxiously from the homestead, "Is that you Johan, Johan?"

He ignored her calls as he did not wish her to see the excellent

4

sporting rifle his father had left in his care. Once the horse had been watered and fed, he removed two loose floorboards in the harness room, wrapped the rifle in oilskin and returned it to its hiding place. He had made certain that none of the Coloured farm workers or kitchen maids had seen him do this.

Johan's mother, Maria, had by now begun to search for him around the farmyard. Her husband had illegally crossed the border of the Cape Colony to join the Boer forces fighting the British Imperial Army, and she had become dependent on Johan, her sixteen-year-old son, for support and protection.

She found him eventually and scolded him roundly for causing her so much anxiety. She had had visions of his being arrested on some feeble pretext. They walked home slowly while he gave her the news of the British patrol's impending arrival. They agreed not to alarm the two younger children, Adrian and Hester, and postponed further discussion until after the evening meal.

The family ate the evening meal in the formal dining room, furnished with yellowwood furniture, polished to a fine patina over many years. The hardwood floors were polished daily and gleamed in the soft light of the oil lamp. The family all held hands and bowed their heads as Maria said grace. The elder of the two Coloured maids, Griet, served the meal: vegetable soup, followed by braised sheep's liver and onions, with preserved peaches and custard for desert.

Once Griet had removed the plates and linen, Maria followed her daily ritual of reading several verses from the Bible, followed by a short prayer — a ritual repeated in almost every Afrikaner home throughout the land. The two maids joined the family for *Skriflesing en Gebed,* but sat quietly to one side on a narrow settee.

Maria had chosen her text to prepare them for tomorrow. The

5

timbre of her voice deepened during her reading, reflecting her resolution to be courageous the next day:

Beware of false prophets, which come
to you in sheep's clothing, but inwardly
they are ravening wolves

She conducted the reading and the concluding prayer in High Dutch, as Afrikaans was not considered sufficiently formal for addressing the Lord. The maids consequently understood the proceedings only partially but sat quietly throughout.

The younger children kissed their mother goodnight and left for bed, lighting their way with home-made candles.

Johan, in a state of great tension, wasted no time in demanding his mother's full attention. "Look, Mother, we have to make a plan and fast. The *Rooinekke* are definitely on their way to steal our horses. The same way they robbed Oom Carel of his hackney stud."

"Slow down, my son. We must think this through carefully. Remember they will issue us with a receipt if they take any of our animals away. We also have to be very careful to hide the fact that your father has crossed the border to join the Boers. They consider that treason."

"Sorry, Mother, Pa would insist we do something if he were here. We must hide the horses — I have a plan."

"Well, let's hear it."

Johan paused to gather his thoughts. "The *Rooinekke* will take several hours tomorrow morning to reach us. Before that, Adrian must take the six thoroughbreds past Leopard Rock and hide them in the nearby kloof. There's water there and they'll be well hidden by the poplar trees. If necessary he could hide them for several days. We must give him blankets and food for at least three days."

"But he's still a child," Maria complained.

"Maybe, but he's an excellent horseman and, more important, he's a Nel!"

Maria was still hesitant. "So what will your part in all this be?"

"I shall take the six hackneys from the stable just after midnight and together with one of the *Volkies*, I'll ride towards the Hantam Mountains, where we can hide for weeks on end if we have to. The hackneys are our lifeblood, Mother. Without them, the farm will collapse. In any case, I can't stand to think that all Father's work will be ruined by these English criminals."

Their discussion went on for several hours before Maria finally agreed to Johan's daring plans. They woke Adrian and explained the plan to him while he listened wide-eyed with excitement. Maria still wanted to send one of the maid's younger brothers with him as a companion and to help with the horses.

But Johan protested. "No, we can't trust the *Volk*. They are scared stiff of their own soldiers who beat them mercilessly to get information." On that note everyone retired to rest, with little hope of much sleep.

During the night the wind direction had changed and a thick mist off the Atlantic enveloped the farmyard and surrounding koppies. Johan and his *Handlanger*, Gert, had left with the hackneys several hours before sunrise. They had no option other than to use a well-defined track leading into the next valley and beyond to the Hantam Mountains. The British patrol would have no problem in following their fresh tracks. Their only hope being the long start they had on the patrol. In spite of the darkness, the horses were behaving well while the two young men encouraged them quietly with the familiar Afrikaans phrases, with which they had been trained as young colts.

Adrian tried to leave with the thoroughbreds shortly after a milky sun had turned the sky to a light grey. But they were skittish in the cool morning air and in the end he had to ask for help from the *Volk* to rope the horses together. Eventually he left with the horses moving in line through the dew-sodden veld. It was too late to carry out his plan of laying a false trail. He had to rely on the stony terrain to cover his tracks, hoping against hope that the volk would not give him away.

Much to the British officer's relief, the stifling heat of yesterday had also dissipated along the valley road. He ordered his men to groom the horses and smarten up their uniforms before leaving. They went about their duties with only half-disguised displeasure, exchanging wisecracks about the officer in their dialect, mostly Afrikaans with a strong infusion of Khoi.

Eventually the tatterdemalion little band moved off at a smart trot, with the officer posting correctly on his cavalry saddle. He was a graduate of Sandhurst, a member of an influential family, but because of an unfortunate indiscretion he had been given this demeaning and exhausting duty. He had deserted his post one night to visit an African prostitute while his regiment was engaged in field exercises. Only his family connections had saved him from a dishonourable discharge. A tough assignment for someone so ambitious to win his spurs in battle.

By the time the patrol reached the homestead it was late morning. Apart from some wispy threads of mist clinging to the cliffs on the koppies, the sun had cleared the sky and warmed the earth, now redolent with the aromas of the desert vegetation.

The party drew up some thirty yards from the homestead, where the officer dismounted and ordered his patrol to remain in place while he led his mount towards the homestead. He halted at the bottom of the steps leading to the front entrance and the wide veranda surrounding the house. As he reached the steps, Maria appeared on the veranda, dressed in her best navy blue woollen dress that reached to her ankles. Her pale blue eyes matched her prematurely grey hair, swept back in an attractive chignon. She was a small, slender figure but her shoulders were squared and her demeanour determined.

The officer removed his white helmet politely, revealing his fair sunburnt skin and tousled blond hair. "Good morning, ma'am. My name is Lieutenant Clarke. I trust you are well and enjoying this excellent day."

Maria replied in heavily accented but fluent, rather stilted English. "Good morning, sir, what can I do for you?"

The officer knew from past experience that it did not pay to beat about the bush with these intolerant Boers and came immediately to the point. "As you know, madam, the British Government, of which the Cape Colony is a part, is engaged in a conflict to bring freedom to all the citizens in the Transvaal and the Orange Free State."

"Freedom, indeed!" she replied.

"Yes, madam, freedom as only we English know and understand it."

"Please get to the point, sir."

"Gladly, I have been instructed by my commanding officer to collect all the horses on this farm for temporary use in Her Majesty's Expeditionary Forces. As you must realise, the horses bred on this farm have earned an enviable reputation in racing circles in Cape Town."

Stunned by the words, "all the horses", Maria gave no sign of it

9

she replied, "We have no horses for you, sir, and I would be greatly obliged if you would leave my property after you have watered your mounts."

"But, madam, you know we always issue co-operating farmers with receipts for the animals we are obliged to commandeer. These can be exchanged in due course for hard cash. Besides, may I ask why I am speaking to you and not the master of this establishment?" His eyes moved around the farmyard with its simple whitewashed buildings and thatched roofs, the sneer on his lip clearly evident.

"My husband is away on business in Cape Town. As you correctly remarked, our horses are well known there and he's visiting clients in the city."

"My orders show that you have two sons. Where are they?"

"They are away in the veld, searching for some stray sheep," she replied.

Clarke had noticed that the sun had moved overhead and did not wish to prolong this frustrating argument. "I am afraid, madam, I must ask you once more to tell me where your horses are kept and, if you do not hand them over to me, I shall be forced to send my men out to find them. In which case you will be contravening Her Majesty's request and I shall not be obliged to issue you with any receipts."

"I repeat, lieutenant, I have no horses for you or for Her Majesty!" Maria replied and turned on her heel to enter the house.

Clarke was now seething with anger, aggravated by the mounting heat and stinging horse flies from the nearby stables. He mounted quickly and led his men to the shade of several large poplar trees, where they started a makeshift camp. A small fire was made to brew tea and cook some oatmeal gruel. The enlisted men grilled the meat of some wild hares that they had snared earlier that week.

The strong sweet tea revived the spirits of the men and they responded enthusiastically to Clarke's orders to ride out and question the *Volk* where the horses had been hidden. The enlisted men were of mixed race: White, Khoi, Bushman and perhaps African. They were tough, wiry and superb trackers. They wasted no time in establishing that the hackneys, plus two riders, had left for the mountains at least ten hours ago. By beating one of the shepherds with whip butts, they found out that the *Kleinbaas* had taken six thoroughbred horses to hide them in the kloof near Leopard Rock.

On receiving this information, Clarke cleared his camp and they all rode out in the direction of the kloof with the bruised shepherd hobbling ahead to show the way.

Adrian had spent the day pleasantly, if somewhat anxiously, below Leopard Rock, skimming stones across the surface of a pond, watching swallows building their mud nests and attending to the horses. He was calmly resting near the pool, admiring the darting flights of the shimmering dragonflies, when he first became aware of danger. The most skittish of the horses, Comet, suddenly lifted his head, pointed his ears and whinnied softly. Adrian then heard men's voices and the sound of hooves on the rocky terrain. There was no way out of the boxed-in kloof; all he could do was calm the animals as best he could and hope they would not find him.

He moved quickly towards Comet, talking to him quietly, while his hand slid up the animal's neck to reassure it. He stroked the warm velvety nose of the horse to quiet its snorting and whickering. Just as he ducked under Comet's neck to move closer to a nearby mare that was becoming nervous, he heard the first crack of a whip. The thoroughbreds immediately started to mill around, kicking up dust and plunging among one another. It was then that he saw the soldier's face through the dust. A wrinkled, wizened face with a scraggly beard and rotten teeth. The first stroke of the whip cut Adrian's legs open; the next spun him around and the third and fourth opened his back. As a second soldier started to beat him with a knopkierie he fainted, his last sensation was of burying his face in the warm Karoo earth.

By the time Clarke stopped his men, Adrian lay limp among the rocks, dust and horse dung.

The patrol took its time moving out of the kloof, leading the splendid thoroughbreds towards the farmyard. It was late afternoon when Clarke rode through the farmyard and onto the valley road without stopping to talk to Maria. He had apparently decided it was not worthwhile to follow the hackneys into the mountains.

As they rode out of the farmyard, the enlisted men spat over their shoulders, cackling with delight and with the expectation that the lieutenant would break out a brandy ration that evening.

Maria immediately dispatched one of the young Coloured boys with a storm lantern to search for Adrian and to tell him that it was safe to return.

It was well into the night before the youngster returned with the news that Adrian lay beneath the overhanging rock in the kloof, covered in blood and dust. Too scared to go any closer, he thought Adrian was dead. The news shocked Maria and it took her several minutes to regain control and start preparations for Adrian's rescue.

She first sent word to the oldest of the farm hands to harness his two donkeys to the smaller of the two donkey carts and come as quickly as possible to the homestead. There, they loaded the cart with an old mattress, blankets, water and a few medicinal supplies before setting out at midnight for the kloof, lighting their way with storm lanterns.

By the time they reached Adrian, the starlight was fading fast and the first rays of the sun had appeared on the eastern horizon. It was light enough to see what a sorry condition the boy was in. He was breathing shallowly. The blood from his wounds had become caked with dust and his clothes were badly torn, exposing extensive abrasions and bruises on his slender legs and torso. His mother wept in anger and frustration as she washed his face and wrapped him gently in a blanket, before carrying him to the cart.

Maria walked and stumbled next to the cart as they slowly made their way home. She held the boy's hand, speaking to him in endearing terms, encouraging him to be brave. *"Hou moed, my liefling,"* "Be brave, my love."

The maids ran out to meet them as they neared the homestead at mid-morning. The elder one, Griet, wept openly. They helped Maria to wash Adrian and to clean his wounds before bandaging him and putting him to bed. He remained unconscious throughout and Maria could not rouse him to take in fluids.

Her next act was to send for her neighbour, Oom Cornelius, some six miles away. He was the lay doctor for the district, setting broken bones and administering home remedies. She also dispatched one of the younger shepherds to track down Johan in the mountains and relay the order to return immediately. He left at a dogtrot with some scanty rations and a steel mirror to use as a crude heliograph in the wild mountain range.

Oom Cornelius arrived late that afternoon. He had ridden hard and his mount was lathered and sweating. He was a small man with a large Old Testament beard and delicate hands. He wasted no time in preliminaries before going straight to Adrian's room. He examined him carefully, flexing each limb in turn and palpating his neck and spine gently. Maria held her breath while he carried out his ex-

13

amination. Eventually he placed his ear against the boy's chest to listen to his heart and breathing.

Looking towards Maria, Cornelius said, "He has no fever yet and none of his bones is broken. These are good signs."

"But what about those terrible cuts from the whips?" she replied.

"I shall leave some salve for the wounds but I fear some of the scars will be there for life. More important, he is dehydrated and you must get fluids into him, even if you have to use a little force. Once he regains consciousness, for which I shall entreat our dear Lord, he will need something for the pain. Use the Jewish peddler's cough mixture. It's full of opium."

Oom Cornelius then asked for a chair and sat for over an hour at Adrian's bedside. Occasionally he closed his eyes in silent prayer and then touched the boy's eyelids lightly. For the most part he just sat quietly, watching his patient.

Maria interrupted his reverie. "Cornelius, it is getting late and you should leave soon. Would you like something to eat before you go?"

"Just some coffee and a few rusks, thank you."

Griet served the coffee for which she was not thanked, and for which she did not expect any thanks. As soon as she had retreated from the room, Oom Cornelius launched into a diatribe of hatred against the English and their filthy Hottentot soldiers; concluding with an admonition to remind Adrian regularly where his scars came from.

Maria's head was swimming with fatigue after Cornelius left. She had just enough strength to put little Hester to bed before collapsing on a mattress next to Adrian's bed. She would wake several times that night to spoon water over Adrian's lips and tongue in an effort to get him to swallow. Early next morning she was rewarded when Adrian swallowed a few spoonfuls of water.

Adrian's recovery was slow and painful but some six weeks later he was again his exuberant self, helping with the farming chores and impishly frustrating his mother's efforts to make him study at home.

2

Oblivious to the humiliation of his younger son, the father of the family, Dirk Nel, was riding at the head of a small commando of twenty men, traversing the short grass prairie of the southern Orange Free State. There had been good rains and the veld grass was succulent and sweet. The horses were in good trim and the commando was making good progress towards joining General Louis Botha, near Colenso.

Dirk always rode at the head of the commando, his eyes searching for landmarks and the best route to follow. The grassy terrain provided an even surface and they were moving at a fast canter. As Dirk was about to give the signal to change to a walk, a small herd of blesbuck appeared on a nearby low hill. Before he could give the signal, a shot rang out from behind and the leading ram staggered to its knees. A second shot bowled it over on its side.

One of the riders had seen the buck before Dirk and had left the group some 500 yards back to drop the animal effortlessly with his Mauser rifle. His name was Du Plessis, and Dirk rode back to discipline him. "Du Plessis, you can't just fire your rifle whenever you bloody well feel like it. This is an army unit and we must maintain strict discipline."

"That may be," Du Plessis answered. "But tonight we are going to eat fresh venison!" Whereupon the whole commando laughed. Dirk knew it was almost impossible to discipline these independent, freedom-loving farmers in a military fashion. So, instead, he grinned rather sheepishly and ordered three men to butcher the animal as quickly as possible. Only the hindquarters and the loin would be kept, the rest left for the jackals.

Once the venison had been made secure on the packhorses, the party continued on its way, searching for an overnight campsite with water and firewood. Nothing nearby appeared suitable, but some two hours later Dirk spotted smoke curling skywards from behind a clump of trees. When they moved closer they saw a small African kraal of about fifteen huts, clustered around some Acacia trees.

As they rode up the women scattered, herding their children into the huts, the air resounding with their cries of alarm and wailing. The African men stood sullenly in small groups, trying to avoid eye contact with the Boers.

Dirk asked to speak to their Headman. There was no response until Du Plessis moved forward and addressed them in surprisingly fluent Zulu. After several exchanges, he told Dirk that the Africans would give them firewood and show them where the spring was. He also added that he had promised them one of the legs of venison. Dirk did not object to Du Plessis' independent bartering; after all he had bagged the venison. Instead, he accepted the arrangements graciously and they rode out to find a suitable campsite.

With the practised eyes of farmers, the commando soon selected a site about two miles from the kraal. The water source was an underground aquifer, which seeped into a vlei, a small marshy area surrounded by reeds and sedges. Just below the vlei was a natural meadow of green kweekgrass, a favourite of the horses.

Dirk moved around the site, quietly giving orders to attend to the horses and weapons before he chose sites for the campfire and for their sleeping quarters. He also appointed the sentries for the night, who would take four-hour watches.

One of the first duties the men tackled was the cutting of veldgrass with sharp sickles, carried by the packhorses. The grass was stuffed into thin canvas bags to provide a little comfort beneath their bedrolls, spread out on the stony ground.

Dirk had to cut his own bedding grass; officers had no special privileges in this voluntary army of farmers.

After he had seen to his night's comfort, Dirk walked some distance away to a rocky outcrop overlooking a wide gully. Here, he discovered that there was a second vlei below him and he rested on the rocky ledge to enjoy the privacy and cool evening air. Golden bishop birds flitted among the bulrushes, their splendid plumage glinting in the late sunlight. There had to be a cliff nearby as dozens of swifts were executing steep turns and darting runs over the surface of the vlei while hawking for flying insects. Close by his rawhide boot he noticed a small gecko, lying spread-eagled to absorb the stored heat from a nearby rock.

The balmy evening and the familiar natural sights and sounds produced a feeling of contentment. He was also pleased that he had been able to lead the commando safely over hundreds of miles. These sentiments were short-lived though, as his thoughts wandered ahead to the battlefield that they would reach within the next few days. Would he measure up to the demands and dangers of conflict? Would his courage desert him and expose him and his family to permanent ridicule? A pang of anxiety gripped him, but eventually passed as he pondered more abstract questions. Had he been right to lead this small commando of Cape rebels away from the safety of their farms to fight the Imperialists? Was he justified in leaving his family in such an isolated area to risk his life on the battlefield? These questions gnawed at him but he soon convinced himself that only God could answer them. He closed his eyes, bowed his head and prayed earnestly while the setting sun finally drained all colour from the African veld.

During Dirk's absence, a small group of Black men appeared at the campsite bearing several loads of firewood. Du Plessis rewarded them with a haunch of venison and half a dozen rolls of tobacco. They were reluctant to leave and curious about the commando. Du Plessis shooed them away unceremoniously, letting them get a good look at his Mauser lying next to his bedroll.

Du Plessis had been the self-appointed cook during their long ride. His energy was limitless. The large, three-legged iron pot was first scrubbed clean in sand and water before placing it directly on the flames to heat rapidly. The kidney fat from the blesbuck ram was then melted in the pot to sear chunks of sizzling venison. After the meat had been browned, salted water was added and once this began to boil, Du Plessis added small potatoes and onions. He then produced his secret reserve of bay leaves and dried herbs, mostly coriander and thyme, to flavour the stew. The aroma was like ambrosia for these hungry young farmers and their tin plates and spoons were soon poised for action. But Du Plessis took pride in his cooking and made them wait until the venison was slowly cooked to a savoury tenderness.

After the meal the young Boers drank a mixture of coffee and chicory out of their tin mugs and most then filled their pipes to enjoy a peaceful smoke beneath the stars.

One of the few men who did not smoke was a tall lean teacher, Michiel Bresler, who hailed from the rural town of Malmesbury, near

Cape Town. He gave his comrades time to finish their smoke, then glanced inquiringly towards Dirk, who nodded his head. This was the signal for Bresler to open his leather-bound Bible and ask for everyone's attention. Bresler had received a sound education at Stellenbosch and read the High Dutch text with a clear and sonorous voice. The reading was, as usual, followed by a short prayer in which Bresler supplicated the Lord to give them strength and courage in the coming battle with the Imperialist forces, bent on robbing them of their country, language and freedom.

For a few moments after the prayer, the men remained silent but conversation soon began to pick up again. Someone remarked on the brilliance of the stars and that gave Bresler the opportunity to point out the major constellations in the southern sky. He gave special attention to the Southern Cross and explained how to find true south by extending the long axis of the cross until it intersected an imaginary line drawn between the two pointers at the side of the Cross. By dropping a perpendicular from the point of intersection to the horizon, one obtained true south.

The young soldiers enjoyed this information as their lives were spent mostly out-of-doors and close to nature. The questions flowed freely and Bresler enjoyed the role of *Meester*, explaining the fundamentals of navigation and how important an accurate chronometer was for establishing longitude. After this explanation one of the men remarked acidly, "Trust the bloody English to claim nought degrees longitude as their own. How arrogant can you get?"

This lightened the mood and Du Plessis was pestered to tell one of his many jokes, "Hey Doep tell us a joke, man!"

The British general and his wife, Mrs. Buller, were often the butt of Du Plessis' humour. He cleared his throat. "Well, see, there was this huge raffle held in Durban for war funds. They didn't tell anyone what the prize was going to be, but the tickets sold like hot cakes. There wasn't a single ou in Durban who hadn't bought one.

"Anyway, the day came for the draw and thousands of those glum-faced Durbanites assembled in the Square to watch the draw. The Mayor climbed on the platform, pulled out a ticket and read out the winner of the third prize. 'Mr. Jackson wins the third prize, which is this fine leather attaché case.' Jackson fetched his prize to the applause of the crowd.

"The Mayor then read out the name of the winner of the second prize, 'Mr. Barker wins the second prize, which is this lovely fruit cake.'

"So Barker walks slowly to the platform, where he confronts the Mayor, 'What the bloody hell's going on? How can you give me only a measly fruit cake as second prize?'

"To which the Mayor replied, 'But it was personally baked by General Buller's wife, Mrs. Buller.'

'Ach! Stuff Mrs. Buller!'

'Sorry, Brother, that's the first prize'"

The men howled with laughter, slapping their knees. Some even had tears in their eyes. Bresler, however, only managed a polite smile and used the occasion to stand up, stretch his lanky frame and announce that it might be wise to turn in as they had some hard riding ahead.

Dirk checked on the sentries, made sure the fires were damped and groped his way in the dark to his bedroll. The highveld air was still balmy; a shrill of crickets was competing with a frog chorus in the vlei while the star tracks wheeled slowly across the sky. As his head came to rest on his old saddle, he looked up at the bright pointers of the Southern Cross. He knew he would only sleep fitfully and each time he woke, the Cross would be in a new position until it came to rest on its head shortly before dawn.

3

Dirk Nel and his commando had made good progress during the past three days and they hoped to join General Botha's forces soon. During the long ride from the Cape Colony they had lost several injured horses. On the previous day they had left two ill and exhausted comrades at a friendly homestead.

On the late afternoon of December 11th they breasted a low hill and finally caught sight of Botha's encampment near Colenso. They cheered spontaneously, waving their rifles above their heads. It had been a long and gruelling ride, but they were proud of their achievement and morale was high in spite of their ragged appearance. Like many Boer soldiers, they had no official uniforms. Most just wore corduroy trousers and jackets, rawhide shoes/*Veldskoene*, large wide-brimmed felt hats and bandoleers of ammunition across their chests. They were all bearded and inured to their own pungent smell of sweat, horses, wood smoke and worn leather.

Dirk led them to an obvious command centre within the encampment. There they were greeted warmly with much vigorous hand-shaking and back-slapping. They were told where to draw stores and find their tents. Dirk was invited to visit Botha's headquarters and a prescient orderly issued them with large cakes of lye soap.

The atmosphere in the camp was surprisingly relaxed and confident. Much of this was due to the Boers' recent impressive victory over the British at Magersfontein. But it was also because of the innate sociable nature of the men. Small groups chatted together, joking and exchanging news about relatives, friends and the condition of their crops and herds. Most of the 8,000 men present, however, were calmly and methodically preparing the defences for an expected British drive through Colenso towards the besieged town of Ladysmith to the north.

Dirk's visit to Botha was brief. The general welcomed him courteously, telling him how much they valued the sacrifices their cousins in the Cape had made to join them. The two men warmed to one another and Botha took the time to explain his strategy for confronting the British attack on Colenso. He instructed Dirk to report the next morning to a Commandant de Wet, who would integrate the Cape commando into the general battle order. Dirk left Botha, realising he had met an exceptional man — handsome and vigorous, with a great deal of energy and confidence.

The following morning Dirk woke early and moved through the adjoining tents to rouse his men. "Move your arses, you lazy bastards, there's work to be done!"

This was greeted with the usual moans, expletives and groans, but after some strong chicory-flavoured coffee and hard rusks, the men became cheerful as they started to banter among themselves.

Commandant de Wet arrived soon after breakfast and issued the men, much to their amazement, with picks and shovels before leading them towards a steep slope overlooking the Tugela River to the south.

When they arrived on the slope they were surprised to see hundreds of their comrades finishing off long trenches, dug into the hillsides. De Wet pointed out a gap in the defences to Dirk and they agreed to entrench the Cape Commando on a slope opposite a northward curving loop in the Tugela River.

Dirk then explained to his men what had to be done and was immediately greeted with good-natured badinage at the prospect of hard labour. Du Plessis was the loudest and insisted jokingly, "I'm not going to dig a trench like a blerrie kaffir, unless I know the reason why."

Dirk looked around to make sure there were no Africans within earshot. Some Boers suspected that they acted as spies for the British. He then called the men together into a closed group to explain Botha's strategy.

"Our leader, Louis Botha, expects that the enemy will try to smash through our defences here at Colenso so that they can break our siege on the town of Ladysmith ten miles to the north. Our comrades have blown up the rail and road bridges across the Tugela. The river is now in flood and the ford to the west has been dug out and destroyed. So we hold some high cards.

"But, as usual, we are outnumbered. If we conceal ourselves carefully, however, in these camouflaged trenches, and remain as quiet as possible, we shall have the advantage of surprise and be able to shoot the shit out of the *Rooinekke.* "

There were general murmurs of approval. Bresler adding piously, "We must also remember that the Lord will be on our side."

Du Plessis showed his appreciation and enthusiasm for the plan by picking up a shovel and saying, "Right, where do we begin?"

They first surveyed the site before starting to dig. They were careful to ensure that they could take cover in the trenches while still being able to enfilade the loop of the Tugela, lying to the south below them.

The morning had begun fresh and cool but the December heat soon began to peak and the men became exhausted, sweat-streaked and covered

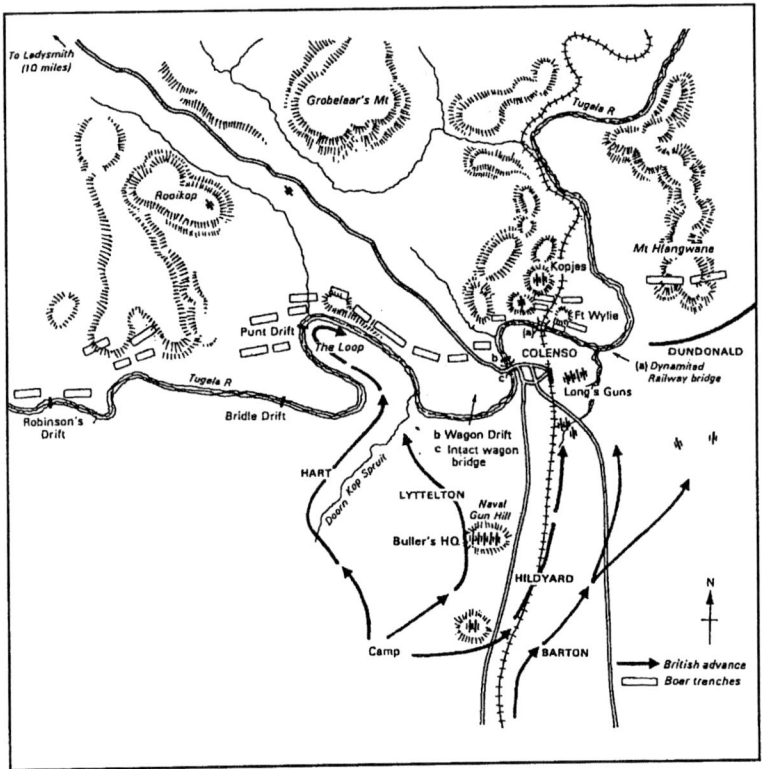

*Battlefield at Colenso showing inter alia: General Buller's head-
quarters, Hart and Hildyard's advances and the Boer trenches. The loop
of the Tugela River into which Hart led his vanguard is north west of
Buller's headquarters.*

*Adapted from: "The Boer War," by Thomas Pakenham (1979).
Randon House, New York.*

in dust. In spite of this, they made good progress and by mid-afternoon Dirk ordered the commando to take a rest and passed around the water bottles. He had dug alongside his men as he was expected to do.

While they rested, de Wet visited them to tell them, "Two of our scouts have just returned from the south. They report that Buller has moved out of Frere with a force of eighteen thousand men. We must be ready for them as soon as possible. *Opskud kêrels!*"

The men renewed their efforts with even greater enthusiasm, urged on by Dirk but prompted also by a frisson of fear in anticipation of the coming battle.

Some 10 miles to the south of Colenso, General Buller's force was moving northwards in well-disciplined groups towards Colenso. He had decided not to go to the assistance of the British forces in the Cape, that desperately needed his help. Instead, he ordered a direct attack on Colenso so that he could relieve Ladysmith by the shortest route. It would turn out to be a calamitous decision by a brave commander, better known for his reckless bravery in winning the Victoria Cross in the Zulu War of 1879, than for his knowledge of military tactics.

Part of Buller's force was the Irish Fifth Brigade, commanded by Major-General Fitzroy Hart. Hart's immediate entourage included a slender young man with a luxurious moustache and sergeant's stripes on his sleeve. His name was Rob McAvoy; he had grown up as a wild youngster in the Belfast slums. When offered the adventure of military service in Africa, he had jumped at the opportunity. During routine training in England an officer had discovered that Rob had an unusual talent. Even with an ordinary service rifle he could shoot with remarkable accuracy. He was removed from his platoon to undergo special training as a marksman and was soon promoted to sergeant.

His duty now was to remain close to Hart during any action and fire on selected targets, picked out by the general or his senior officers. Hart became fond of Rob; he was impeccably neat, cared lovingly for his custom-made Lee-Enfield rifle and was always cheerful and respectful. Characteristics that his mother in Belfast would be surprised to learn.

On the evening of December 14th, Buller's army was positioned for its assault on the Boer forces. He received his senior officers in his usual patrician style to explain his final plan of attack. "Look here, gentlemen, the position is actually quite clear. We outnumber the Boers almost two to one and, according to our scouts, they are milling around in their usual unorganised fashion. We shall therefore seize the opportunity to carry out a direct attack as soon as possible." It was typical of the man; simple, straightforward and unimaginative. He had decided to attack the Boers head on with two brigades and force his way across the river. On the eastern flank, his mounted brigade was to attack the Boers positioned on the Hlangwana koppie.

Before dawn on December 15th the Boers silently entered their trenches on the hillsides overlooking Colenso. It was a cool, delightful morning once again. The dawn chorus of bird song would soon begin at the river's edge below. But nothing could have been farther from the thoughts of the men about to be joined in battle.

At exactly 5.30 am Buller's heavy artillery thundered to life at a range of three miles. The exploding shells ripped up great spouts of earth but inflicted few casualties on the Boers, who remained quietly in the shelter of their trenches.

Tension in the trenches was, however, mounting. Du Plessis

worked the bolt on his rifle noisily and impatiently. The success of Botha's strategy required absolute quiet in the trenches and Dirk lost his temper. He leaned across Bresler, sitting next to him, and in a loud whisper addressed Du Plessis, "Doep, you bastard, if you make another sound, I'll personally come over there and cut out your *Knaters*".

Du Plessis reddened with embarrassment but still managed a good-natured smile for his commander.

Colonel Long of Omdurman fame had been put in charge of the heavy field guns on the eastern flank of the British thrust. His explicit orders were to move the guns closer to the Boer entrenchments but at all costs to remain outside the range of small-arms fire. To Buller's astonishment and chagrin, Colonel Long and his men manoeuvred the guns to within a few hundred yards of the river.

No sooner had they got the guns positioned, when Botha's great Krupp howitzer fired a single reverberating shot. This was the signal the Boers had been waiting for. Withering rifle fire immediately raked across Long's detachment. Within minutes 30 per cent of the men became casualties. Long, himself badly wounded, ordered his men to abandon the guns and they retreated out of range of the enemy's deadly accurate fire.

Meanwhile an even more disastrous action was taking place on the western flank. Fitzroy Hart's Irish Fifth Brigade was marching in close order towards the ford to the west of the loop in the Tugela River. Hart was a stickler for old-fashioned military precision and insisted that his brigade march in close order towards the river as if they were on the parade ground.

At 6.15 am they reached a point some 300 yards from the start of the northward curving loop in the river. The ford, where they were meant to cross the river was to the left of the loop but Hart's African guide, who could scarcely speak English, insisted that it was near the apex of the loop.

Hart agreed and ordered his troops to march into the salient formed by the loop. A dangerous military decision in any circumstances, especially so because Hart still had time to turn back to extricate his force. In fact, a young cavalry officer riding hell for leather past their left flank shouted repeatedly, "Turn back while you can. The Boers are in trenches across the river, ready to mow you down. Go back! Go back!" Despite these warnings, Hart ordered his men forward.

The Boers entrenched above the loop in the Tugela also responded to Botha's howitzer signal. Their enfilading fire ravaged the packed ranks of Hart's brigade. Many broke ranks to take cover, some refused to go forward, but Hart and his officers courageously urged them forward into the salient and many more were ruthlessly and systematically cut down. Within 40 minutes 400 men had been either killed or severely wounded. Eventually the brigade started to retire, leaving hundreds of dead and dying. The dead, silent in their bloodstained khakis, were mute testimony to the crass stupidity of a brave but pompous officer.

Rob McAvoy had kept close to Hart during the early stages of the action, but as soon as the vanguard of the brigade started to fall, he took cover, nursing his beloved Lee-Enfield. As the action began to die down and the retreat began in earnest, he raised his head to survey the slope above the loop.

He soon noticed a sharp point of glinting light directly above the loop. It was Dirk's brass telescope flashing in the early morning sun. Rob crept forward to a nearby tree stump and, while crouching next to the stump, he used it as a dead rest to aim carefully at the dark shape next to the pinpoint of light.

Rob's bullet entered Dirk's forehead just above his right eyebrow, smashing through his cerebellum before being deflected downwards to the brainstem. He fell back violently, his body convulsing from the fatal injury.

Unlike the Boers, Rob was not using smokeless cartridges and within 20 seconds three high-velocity bullets slammed into his body. One of them had been fired by Du Plessis, who could fell a springbok at 400 yards with ease. Rob died instantly.

Bresler, still next to Dirk, gathered his fallen comrade in his arms, oblivious to the blood running over his hands and face. He comforted the already dead commander. *"Hou moed ou vriend, ons staan by jou,"* "Courage, dear friend, we are with you."

By now Buller had decided to cut his losses and concentrate on rescuing his field artillery. During the rescue operation heavy losses were again incurred and five Victoria Crosses were awarded to the courageous volunteers. Lieutenant Roberts, the son of Lord Roberts was severely wounded in this action and left for hours in the hot sun until the Boers chivalrously returned him. He died later that night and Lord Roberts, who later became supreme commander of the British forces in South Africa, never forgave Buller for abandoning his son.

Buller finally called off the action at 8 am. Jubilation spread through the Boer ranks, many of whom were still not sure if they could leave their cover to take prisoners and rout the retreating enemy.

In contrast, the Cape commando was stunned by the loss of their beloved comrade. Bresler continued to rock him in his arms. Doep laid down his rifle and sobbed openly. He wept for the loss of his commander, but also for the loss of his own innocence as he surveyed the butchery on the battlefield through a haze of cordite fumes and the dust off the African veld.

The Queen's surgeon, Dr. Treves, was horrified by the carnage. Scores of horribly wounded men, burnt by the sun, screamed in pain as his assistants laboured into the night amputating limbs, stitching wounds and finally covering the dead with tarpaulins as it began to rain.

Botha telegraphed Pretoria on December 15th, "Today the God of our fathers has given us a great victory."

Dirk had died ignorant of the humiliating beating, endured by his favourite son, Adrian.

4

It took more than ten days for the news of Dirk's death to reach the farm in Calvinia. The dominee brought the news, driving out in his smart spider drawn by a chestnut gelding. As usual, he was dressed in black broadcloth in spite of the summer heat.

Nothing could have prepared him for Maria's total collapse. He had to stay overnight and send for the neighbour's wife to comfort her. No one could rouse her from a deep depression. Eventually they had to leave her closeted in her room with Griet doing her best to help.

When Johan heard of his father's death, he ran sobbing from the room. Some hours later he saddled up one of the hackneys and rode off in the direction of the Hantamberge. He carried his father's Mauser rifle slung openly across his back. Adrian turned pale with shock but did not break down immediately. He turned first to his mother for comfort. When she ignored him, he climbed into bed and wept copiously.

Little Hester eventually realised she would no longer be able to sit on her father's lap and be tickled by his bushy beard, as he smoked his pipe and told her stories about wild animals. She was confused and bewildered by her mother's behaviour and ran to Griet for sympathy, who cradled her and sang to her as she had when Hester was still an infant.

Maria's depression persisted for weeks; her behaviour became increasingly strange as she took to taking long walks in the veld. Her long skirts became tattered at the hem, her shoes were broken and dirty and her usual immaculate neatness was replaced by an eccentric untidiness. At dusk the farm hands could see her gaunt figure outlined against the horizon, her skirts flaring in the wind, evoking an elemental uneasiness among them.

Johan returned to the homestead after living rough for several days in the mountains. His demeanour was serious, determined and somewhat arrogant. He ignored his mother's collapse and took over the organisation of the farm, giving Adrian and Hester important chores around the homestead. He gave orders to Griet gruffly, without a please or thank you. She responded respectfully and her devotion to the routine housekeeping kept the family together. Johan did his best to reinforce this semblance of ordinary life by leading the family in scripture reading and prayers every evening after supper.

Occasionally Johan saddled the bay mare in the late afternoon to ride off in the direction of Calvinia. He remained away all night, and never gave any explanation of where he had been. On these evenings Griet made the two youngsters clasp their hands together after supper and recite the Lord's Prayer, *Onse Vader.*

The unreal quality of their changed lives lasted well into February when it became clear to Johan that the very fabric of their family life was threatened.

One afternoon he returned early from tending the sheep and strode through the farmhouse to his mother's bedroom. He knocked loudly on the door and was rewarded with a faint, *"Kom binne."*

Immediately after entering, he confronted his mother, "Moeder, I'm sorry but I must speak to you seriously." Maria turned a wan face to him but did not reply.

Johan's frustration was rising and he addressed his mother forcibly, even abandoning the polite 'you'. "You cannot go on like this. You are behaving shamefully and dragging the name of our family through the mud. Where is your courage? Where is your respect and love for our father, who gave his life for our volk? I'm ashamed of you."

Maria continued to stare distractedly out of the window and Johan's anger overwhelmed him as he left the room, slamming the door. He did not attend the family supper that evening. Instead, he rode off in the direction of town without greeting anyone.

After the outburst in Maria's room, Hester fled to Griet who comforted her and Adrian by making them their favourite dessert and putting them to bed early.

The next morning Adrian rose early and dressed quickly in his khaki shorts and shirt before going down the passage towards the kitchen. On entering he was surprised and then overjoyed to see his mother busying herself over the stove, together with Griet. She turned to him, her pale blue eyes searching his face. "Good morning, my child, did you sleep well?" She asked. "We are making *Pannekoek* so that we can all enjoy a special breakfast."

Adrian did not know what to say, but Hester broke the ice by running through the door and flinging herself into her mother's arms, while Griet giggled with pleasure. The two youngsters then sat quietly together as they watched the making of the crepes.

Maria first sifted the white flour and then, using a beaten egg and small amounts of milk and water, prepared a soft batter, to which she added melted butter. She then greased her large cast-iron skillet, heated it on the old Dover stove and dropped large spoonfuls of the batter on the sizzling skillet. When it started to bubble, Maria turned the crepe over and cooked it until it became a light golden brown. After rolling it up she sprinkled it with sugar and cinnamon before serving it.

The warmth of the stove and the fragrance of the cinnamon spread through the kitchen; and it was this scene, together with the smiling faces, that greeted Johan as he entered the back door in his dishevelled clothes. His expression changed immediately. He went quickly to Maria's side, bent over her and kissed her affectionately, his eyes filling with tears.

Her children's love, and the many pleasures she enjoyed on the farm, sustained Maria's recovery. She enjoyed working in her vegetable and fruit garden; two acres of irrigated flat land, about two hundred yards from the homestead.

Here she had planted plum, peach and apple trees that could survive the winters of Calvinia. She preserved surplus summer fruit in glass jars and stored them in a dark pantry. The large patch of bright green lucerne, she cut and fed to her flock of Golden Australops. They rewarded her in turn with large brown eggs with bright yellow yolks. Pumpkins and fancy gourds grew in profusion. After harvesting, Maria stored them on the corrugated iron roof of an old shed. She used the gourds for holding sour milk as it thickened and fermented into *Kalbasmelk,* similar to a liquid yoghurt. Cauliflower, radishes, carrots and cabbage all did well but Maria took special delight in her herbs. Their modest flowers and subtle fragrances intrigued her. Winter frosts killed off the herbs so she harvested them in autumn, drying them in muslin bags, hung from the beams in the barn. Her favourites were basil, or *Koningskruid*, mint, marjoram, rosemary and lemon thyme, or *Sitroentiemie.*

She worked long hours in her garden, assisted by two of the

farm hands, while Adrian and Hester usually played close by; paddling in the irrigation furrow, making boats out of twigs, stealing young carrots and telling each other stories.

Soon after Maria's recovery she decided it was time to face the townspeople, her attorney and above all to attend church. *Nagmaal/* Communion was to be celebrated on the first Sunday in March and she sent word to her older cousin, Sarah, in the village that she and the children would stay over on that weekend.

Preparations for the visit entailed checking Sunday-best clothes, altering Dirk's shirts to fit Johan, who was developing into a powerful young man and preparing simple gifts for relatives and friends in town.

Maria discussed their transport arrangements with Johan. "Shall we take the spider as well as the wagon?" She asked. "We can then use the spider for visiting friends and the wagon for the heavy supplies. We must have some wheat milled, our flour is running out and we need paraffin, salt, vinegar and much more.

"We could do that, Ma, but who would drive the spider? The only hackney that pulls it easily is Blits. He has a hard mouth and is difficult to handle."

"Adrian could, I've been watching him. He seems to have a way with horses."

"Never, he's far too skinny and unsure of himself. The four of us will go in the Cape Cart and arrive with some dignity. I'll take the wagon in next week with a few volk to collect the supplies."

Maria deferred to Johan. Her grief was still too close to the surface to risk a confrontation with her elder son, who was becoming increasingly authoritarian. Instead, she turned to the problem of making a long black dress in the Victorian style for Hester to wear to church. She would also make the black arm bands and neck ties for the boys while preparing her own widow's weeds meticulously.

The following Saturday the family set out in the Cape Cart for Calvinia. Maria and Johan sat up front, with the two youngsters squeezed in the back between the luggage and gifts of farm produce. Maria wore a simple dustcoat over her formal dress as the horses' hooves raised clouds of dust with every step. This eventually covered all the passengers and the luggage. A three-hour bumpy drive lay ahead of them but they all shared a cheerful sense of expectancy. Johan had polished the harness and tied red ribbons to the bridles. He had fed the horses a liberal amount of *Dagga*/marijuana, along with their hay and they were high stepping and arching their necks. The cadence of the clicking hooves and the steady jingling of the harness soon lulled everyone into a pleasant reverie as they watched the familiar landscape pass slowly by.

As they entered the town, Johan used his buggy whip expertly to keep the horses pulling smoothly with a showy gait, urging them on, *"Kom Oubaas se perde! Kom, kom kom julle beauties!"*

The two youngsters had not been to town for many months and gazed excitedly about, chattering together. Maria and Johan sat upright, looking straight ahead, keenly aware that onlookers would recognise and identify them as a bereaved family. Their arrival at Cousin Sarah's home was, nevertheless, a joyful reunion with much hugging, kissing and voices raised in a babble of welcoming sounds.

Maria produced her gifts of farm produce — a leg of lamb, dried spiced sausage, farm butter, eggs and a variety of fresh vegetables. Everyone then retired to a shady veranda, where Sarah's Coloured maids served weak milky tea in the Afrikaner style, together with a lemon-flavoured sponge cake and a fig preserve in its own delectable syrup. Maria greeted the maids politely but did not breach protocol by asking after their health. She would do so later when helping in the kitchen.

Soon after tea Johan disappeared, much to his mother's concern. He did not return until late that night.

The next morning the two families walked to the Dutch Reformed Church and, as requested by the dominee, occupied the front pew.

Dominee Louw, a tall well-built man with a shock of grey hair, shook hands with each member of the Nel family as he made his way to the pulpit, high above the congregation. He announced the first hymn, *Prys den Heer met Blyde Galm,* and the organist, Aunt Betsie Steenkamp, massaged the wheezing organ into life. The congregation joined in at such a dragging tempo that Aunt Betsie had to slow down her rendering of the famous hymn. It soon sounded more like a dirge than an anthem and the final chords brought welcome relief to Maria who had studied music at Stellenbosch.

The dominee's strong ringing voice soon restored a mood of anticipation for the ritual of communion. He welcomed the congregation with the time-honoured phrases, "Brothers and Sisters, we are gathered in the sight of God to celebrate His communion with our sinful souls and to bow our heads in deep gratitude for His many blessings."

After communion and several lengthy readings from the scriptures, the dominee cleared his throat noisily and began his sermon. He started quietly, exploring the meaning of his text and its bearing on the life of their farming community. He then lowered his voice to express the congregation's sympathy with the Nel's tragic loss of the head of their family, emphasising how proud they were of his supreme sacrifice for the Boerevolk. This then led to a systematic condemnation of the British government and its exploitation of the Afrikaner volk. By this time the rhythm of delivery had picked up and his voice rose to a crescendo as he thumped the lectern with each admonition of the evils perpetrated by the British.

Maria became embarrassed and kept her gaze on her folded hands. Hester felt frightened as the dominee's delivery reached its climactic heights and she reached for her mother's hand. Adrian was more interested in watching a puppy playing outside, but Johan was electrified by the sermon. He sat bolt upright, his eyes fixed on the pulpit.

As the two families returned to Sarah's home, they chatted about the weather and made inconsequential comments about members of the congregation. They avoided any reference to the sermon, fully realising how sensitive and disruptive Afrikaner politics could be. Johan strode ahead in sullen silence.

The mood soon became cheerful on arrival at the house as the women and maids began to prepare Sunday dinner. The men sipped small goblets of sweet white wine on the veranda while the finishing touches were being made to the dinner. This was served at a long table in the formal dining room. Roast lamb and a chicken pie provided the main course together with roast potatoes, onions, fresh green peas, yellow rice, studded with sultanas, and pumpkin fritters strewn with cinnamon sugar. The dessert was Sarah's special milk tart, flavoured with coconut and served with thick clotted cream.

Sunday, a day of rest, allowed the adults to nap in the afternoon with a clear conscience, in spite of their sinful over-indulgence at dinner. The youngsters, as usual, had been warned of the dire consequences that would befall them if they so much as made a peep on the Sabbath afternoon. In spite of this, they sneaked out of the house and played in the cool shade of a small vineyard and an old peppercorn tree in the back yard. Hester made clay animals near the duck pond, while Adrian entertained his young cousins with frightening stories about leopards in the Hantamberge.

Next morning Maria dressed again in her widow's weeds to visit her attorney, Jean du Toit, with Johan. As she expected, Dirk's will stipulated that his entire estate was to be left to his elder son, Johan, but she would retain the income until he reached his majority. This did not upset her but she was shocked by the size of the mortgage on the farm and the large interest payment due in July.

They both left Meneer du Toit's office with a sense of foreboding. Maria tried to comfort Johan saying, "Don't worry, son, we'll manage somehow. With faith, the Lord will provide."

"Forget the Lord, Ma; we'll have to help ourselves. The mortgage was used to buy the thoroughbreds that the Goddamned British stole from us. We must get our own back one day."

"Ach, Johan, it won't help to dwell on that right now. We must arrange for the shearers to come to the farm next week. Let's pray that the wool clip will cover this year's mortgage payment, with a little to spare. Please see to it straight away, son. I'm going to Jan Brand's store to order our supplies."

The Nels returned to the familiarity of the homestead with relief. The pleasant routine on the farm: tending the horses and sheep and cultivating the fruit and vegetable garden took on a rhythm of its own, while Maria's love and self discipline provided the pivot for their closely knit family life.

Johan had not been able to get the shearers until late March. This meant that the shorn sheep faced the risk of an early winter storm.

But they had no choice. In the meantime he persuaded his mother that they should thresh the wheat, which was now lying in tall stacks of bound sheaves next to the threshing floor.

Wheat growing was a gamble in the arid climate of Calvinia. Success depended on good winter rains. Lucky last year; the Nels had gathered a good harvest from their bottom field that held moisture well.

Johan was an experienced thresher and organised a team of farm hands for the task, including Adrian, before leaving for town. The threshing floor consisted of a circular floor of hard-packed earth, enclosed by a low stone wall. The sheaves were packed three deep around the inside perimeter of the wall. One man, Japie, stood in the centre of the floor, holding the long rein attached to the lead mule in one hand and a horsewhip in the other. Japie's careful pressure on the long rein and accurate whipping kept a team of mules trotting continuously over the sheaves. Another man, Kerneels, using a pitchfork, made sure the sheaves remained beneath the hooves of the trotting mules. Japie's job was the most difficult. The trick was not to whip the mules too hard as they would panic and stumble over one another. Most often the whip cracked well above their hides and only occasionally *pietsed* them on the rump to let them know who was boss. Kerneels's job was less demanding but he had to move quickly to stay out of range of the vicious hooves of the mules as his pitchfork rearranged the sheaves.

After the sheaves had been reduced to a mixture of chaff and grain, they were tossed into the air, allowing the wind to remove the chaff while the heavier grain fell to the floor. The notorious south easter in summer could usually be relied on to do this efficiently.

Adrian's job was to pitch sheaves from the stack towards the

42

threshing floor. He hated the work, his hands became blistered and the chaff dust collected under his shirt and itched like hell. Soon after their lunch break, Adrian was resting on his pitchfork, watching the mules trotting in fine style over a new batch of sheaves when, suddenly, Kerneels screamed in panic. A mule had kicked him hard on the upper arm and, as Adrian watched, Kerneels fell forward and lay quite still. One of the following mules had accidentally kicked a glancing blow to his head.

Adrian's mouth went dry and his heart began to race as he shouted to Japie to stop the mules. This was easier said than done as the animals were alarmed by Japie's panic-stricken cries; they laid their ears back milled around the floor, kicking out wildly. Adrian walked along the top of the low stone wall, took the long rein from Japie and pulled the lead mule towards him while speaking calmly to the other animals and leading them away from Kerneels's body. He shouted to Japie to open the gate and led the mules to a nearby kraal, where he and Japie calmed them further and let them loose.

Adrian and Japie ran back to the threshing floor to find that the other men had poured water over Kerneels's head and that he had come round, but was still writhing in pain. They all looked to Adrian to take over. He knelt over the small pitiful figure, sobbing in pain, dressed in cast off clothes, little better than rags. He sent Japie to fetch Maria, "Fetch the *Nooi* quickly. Tell her to bring bandages and cotton wool. Run!"

The other men brought an old door from a nearby stable and they did their best to make Kerneels comfortable on it, using straw bedding.

His face was still contorted with pain when Maria arrived. She knelt over him, washed and bandaged the cut on his forehead. After spooning a mixture of brandy and the morphine-rich cough-mixture into his mouth, she discovered that his upper arm was badly fractured. She then organised a small group to carry Kerneels to his little thatched hut, after sending Adrian to fetch the bonesetter, Oom Cornelius.

The bonesetter arrived after sunset and Adrian had to lead him to Kerneels's hut by lamplight. The thatched hut consisted of two rooms, one with a large hearth. As they entered, the odour of unwashed bodies, rancid fat, wood and tobacco smoke enveloped them. This did not seem to disturb Cornelius whose expression was largely hidden behind his apostolic beard. He moved quickly to kneel at Kerneels's bedside, seemingly oblivious of the stench and grime. Adrian held the lamp above the patient and marvelled at the skill of the bonesetter's hands and the tender way in which he spoke to Kerneels. Shortly before he had been berating all Coloureds as lazy thieving *Hotnots*. Now he slowly straightened Kerneels' arm and carefully secured it in a set of wooden splints that he had crafted himself. When finished, he turned to Kerneels's diminutive wife and gave her instructions on how to care for her husband, leaving an extra bottle of painkiller behind. She clasped her hands together and thanked him profusely, "Thank you, master, may the Lord bless you and keep you."

Adrian and Oom Cornelius washed at the homestead, where Cornelius received his fee of five shillings from Maria. He told Maria what a help Adrian had been; "Yes, he deserves at least half this fee. I also noticed that he has the famous Nel hands. Who knows, he may follow in my footsteps one day?"

Adrian was embarrassed by the compliment but his experience with the bonesetter had clearly affected him.

Soon after the threshing was over, a gang of shearers arrived to shear the Nel's flock of merinos. The men were housed in the harness room and Maria and Griet prepared big pots of rich mutton stew and large loaves of whole wheat bread to feed the men. Griet always served the food to them; Maria never even spoke to them. Johan urged everyone to work as quickly as possible so that the sheep could at least produce a short fleece before the notorious Calvinia winter descended on them. The teamwork of the shearers, the wool sorters and shepherds made short shrift of the task. After only two weeks, Johan loaded the wagon with the first bales of the season's clip to take to town. He was well satisfied with the quality of the wool — long, well-crimped fibres with a clean stylish appearance. The shearers accompanied him on the wagon, nursing their hangovers from the previous evening's binge on cheap *Vaal Japie*. The foreman complained to Johan, "My Gawd, Master, my head is so blerrie sore I can't even touch my hair."

Adrian was left behind to clear up the mess in the shearing shed. It had not taken long and he was enjoying a lazy moment, lying on top of a wool bale, watching the barn swallows knifing through the dappled light that filtered through chinks in the thatch. Dust motes glinted in the shafting light while that most African of sounds, the soft calling of turtle doves, reached Adrian from the loft. During these reflective moments he often thought of his father and sometimes ended up weeping inconsolably. But this morning he daydreamed about the thoroughbreds they had lost and how he would recapture them from the British in a daring raid and return them to the farm. He had grown deeply attached to the horses, especially to Comet, the bay gelding, that could gallop as though ten devils were after him whenever he gave him his head.

A sharp call from the homestead broke into his reverie and he remembered his promise to Maria to do some schoolwork this morning.

He returned to the homestead to find that Maria had spread out the books and scribblers on the dining room table. Maria had obtained unofficial permission from the local principal, Meneer van Wyk, to keep the boys temporarily out of school because of Dirk's death and the turmoil caused by the war. He was an old friend of the family and loaned her study materials for both boys. Johan, being older had received most of his formal schooling before the war. He now refused to do any studying but was occasionally caught reading one of the textbooks on the sly. Once he got down to it, Adrian enjoyed the schoolwork with his mother. But his real interest lay in art and he could draw remarkably well for someone who was self-taught.

A few of the books on the table were in high Dutch. Most were in English, none was in Afrikaans. Maria opened the English grammar text and asked Adrian to correct the faulty phrases.

"What is wrong with, 'that's him'?" She asked.

"It should be, 'that is he'."

"What about, 'that's her'?"

"It should be, 'that is she'. But, Ma, nobody talks like that, not even the English teacher's children."

"It doesn't matter, you must get it right. Come now, concentrate!"

Adrian endured another hour of this tedium, knowing that his mother would eventually switch to reading one of the well known English or Dutch novels aloud. This morning they were going to read *Treasure Island*, one of his favourites.

Their mutual enjoyment of the reading was interrupted by Griet, who announced that the *Smous*, the Jewish peddler, had arrived on the farm. This was always cause for excitement as his small wagon was full of surprises and small treasures, apart from mundane household essentials. Maria let him bunk in the harness room and invited him to have coffee and rusks in the kitchen. His social standing did not warrant an invitation into the front room. That was reserved for neighbours, the dominee and relatives from town.

Maria greeted the smous cheerfully, "Good morning, Mister Freeman. How are you keeping? What a terribly hot day to be travelling. Please sit down and Griet will serve us coffee."

Freeman replied in fairly fluent Afrikaans, richly laced with Yiddish words. "Thank you, madam. I'm very pleased to accept your hospitality."

Maria enjoyed Freeman's visits. He passed on gossip about the district and seemed very knowledgeable about national politics and the course of the war. They chatted amiably for almost an hour, before she accompanied him to his small wagon, where he showed her his latest acquisitions.

Maria knew she spent too much on these occasions but she enjoyed Freeman's dry wit and entertaining news. She stocked up on the famous analgesic cough mixture, Epsom salts, bicarbonate of soda, castor oil in small blue bottles, needles, thread, various spices, some sweets and a collection of small toys for Hester's next birthday. She also left scissors and knives with Freeman for repair and sharpening. With his mother's permission, Adrian cleaned out his savings and with great excitement bought a brand new Joseph Rogers penknife.

Later that evening the workers would flock around Freeman's wagon and barter with their few coins, tied tightly in old handkerchiefs, for his seductive trinkets.

The farm hands were paid a pittance. To partly compensate, they received a generous allowance of flour and mutton each week, a dozen dried fish, or *Bokkems*, a little milk for infants and every evening a bottle of dry white wine. During the day they were given a tot of wine on rising, then at breakfast and at lunch. There was no schooling for the children and medical attention was usually limited to what the farmer's wife could provide. Neighbouring farmers, including the Nels, cooperated to build small thatched churches for the labourers, who were mostly devout Christians. Although few could read, some could recite long texts from the Bible by heart.

Much to Johan's relief winter was late that year. The sheep had had time to grow a reasonable fleece to ward off the cold. The cold fronts off the South Atlantic had been mild but had brought welcome rain, transforming the arid veld into a floral paradise. When their work allowed it, Maria took the boys on long walks through the veld, teaching them some basic botany while revelling in the superb display of desert flowers.

"Look here, Adrian," she would exclaim. "This is an exquisite example of a *Kalkoentjie*, it belongs to the Gladiolus genus. Isn't it lovely?"

The boys would nod respectfully and murmur agreement. They shared their mother's delight in the explosion of Namaqualand daisies that ran like rivers of gold between the austere greys and dark greens of the perennial desert shrubs. But it was considered unmanly to wax too poetic about their beauty. In the marshy areas bright yellow bulbinellas bloomed in profusion and Arum lilies could be picked by the armful. These outings helped Maria face the shock and loneliness resulting from Dirk's death, but she could not rid herself of a gnawing uneasiness about the mortgage payments on the farm and Johan's unpredictable behaviour.

On returning from the most recent of these walks, Maria addressed the boys, "This morning the first frost nipped our vegetable garden. Next week the heavy frosts will start in earnest. I told Griet we will take all our meals in the kitchen from tomorrow and that she must keep the stove burning all day."

Johan agreed, "Yes, Ma, you will have to let Adrian off school for a few days so that he can help us herd the sheep down to the Onderveld, where they will have more protection against the north westers. Pa used to do it at this time every year."

"Yes, Boet, I know. You will also have to plan a springbok hunt. The buck will be moving away for the winter and we will soon need a good supply of *Biltong*/jerky."

"*Ja-Nee.*"

The sheep trek to the Onderveld went smoothly, mainly thanks to Johan's strict discipline and Adrian's skilful handling of the horses and kelpie sheepdogs. They returned exhausted, wind-burnt and smelling of horse sweat, ripe corduroy and sheep dung. Maria made Griet heat several paraffin tins of water on the stove and they took it in turns to bathe in large zinc tubs in front of the glowing cast iron stove. Maria retired modestly from the kitchen when the boys stripped for their baths, but Griet remained to help with the pouring of water and handing out towels and soap. It was as though she was not a real person.

Later that week, after prayers, Johan produced pencil and paper to plan their springbok hunt. They would be away for several days and require food, warm clothing, blankets, cooking pots, sharp knives and, naturally, rifles and ammunition — both black-market items.

Maria also insisted on a first-aid kit.

Maria pointed out the advantages of taking a small wagon, as their father had done, to hold all their gear and provide shelter for sleeping.

But Johan disagreed, "We'll have to cross rough ground to reach the springbok. A wagon will only be a nuisance and slow us down. I vote for two pack mules and Adrian and I will each ride a hackney."

As usual Johan got his way and early the following week the two brothers left on the hunt. They were dressed in long corduroy pants, long woollen socks, veldskoene, sheepskin jackets and wide-brimmed felt hats. They each led a neatly packed mule and their excitement was obvious from the way they sat their horses and shared their laughter. Little Hester was also caught up in the excitement as she lifted her long skirt and ran part of the way next to the horses, her braids bouncing on her shoulders. She worshiped her brothers but Maria suspected she had a special fondness for Adrian.

For the next several hours the boys kept up a steady walk across a wide plain until they spotted the family's flock of goats, grazing on the slope of a small rocky koppie. There, as expected, they met the old goatherd, Gert, who greeted them effusively, his brown wrinkled face creased with pleasure as he grinned toothlessly at them. *"Dag, master, hoe gaan dit met master?"* He enquired.

Johan used the respectful term of *Outa* to answer Gert, "It goes well, Outa, how goes it with Outa?"

"Nay, master, not so good. I lost a young *Bokkie* to that blerrie lynx last night. If I catch the bastard, I'll cut out his *Knaters!*"

"What would that help, Outa? He doesn't hump the goats, he eats them."

Gert dissolved in laughter as Johan and Adrian dismounted to walk through the flock. They had not inspected it for several weeks. The animals were in good condition and feeding greedily on the herbs and grasses, brought on by the rains. Most of the ewes were pregnant and would kid in the spring.

Johan gave Gert some tobacco, a little food and some farm remedies for the goats. Gert shuffled his feet in a little dance in thanks for each item and stuffed them into his two haversacks, made from goatskin and jackal pelts. Before leaving, Johan enquired about the movement of the springbok. "Outa, when did you last see the springbok?"

"Master, only last week I saw a large herd on the other side of Renosterkop. Master must ride through the Doringkloof so as not to spook them. They'll make really *lekker* biltong. They're as fat as zebras."

Renosterkop was in the direction of the Hantamberge and about two days' ride away. The boys settled into their saddles, spoke encouragingly to their mounts and left Gert to his goats and the desolate landscape.

By evening they reached a steep cliff face at the mouth of a canyon known as Doringkloof. The cliff would provide shelter against the cold wind and there was a plentiful supply of firewood in the kloof. Johan collected the wood while Adrian knee-haltered the horses and mules before turning them loose to graze. It took some time to clear a comfortable space for their bedrolls, but before long everything was in place and a crackling fire was blazing as the sun set swiftly behind the cliff.

Johan fancied himself as an outdoor cook. As soon as the burning wood had produced glowing coals, he brushed a heap of coals beneath a wire grill and laid the salted lamb ribs on the sizzling grill.

Meanwhile Adrian tore chunks off a fresh brown loaf and put the coffeepot on to boil. They ate heartily and enjoyed the steaming coffee as they watched the stars increase in brilliance overhead. Jackals were keening in the distance, while owls duetted high above on the cliff.

Long before dawn, the boys rose from their uncomfortable beds to breakfast on strong coffee and hard rusks. It was bitterly cold and the frost crunched beneath their rawhide boots. The cold and black night seemed to have sharpened the edges of the diamond-hard stars. They shivered beneath the vastness of the night sky.

Their early start paid off and they arrived at Renosterkop earlier than expected. The south easter had blown away the thick cumulus by noon and the welcome sun felt good on their backs. Johan called a halt when they left the kloof and reached a steep rise overlooking a narrow valley. He crawled forward quietly and soon signed to Adrian not to follow him.

When he got back he reported sighting a fairly large herd of springbok and he and Adrian returned to the kloof to hide the horses and mules. They filled their pockets with ammunition and checked the bolts and sights on their rifles. Johan was using his father's powerful Mauser, while Adrian had to be content with a Winchester point 22.

They leopard-crawled up the rise until they could just see over the rim. Their khaki-coloured floppy hats camouflaged them well. Johan could hardly contain his excitement. He turned to Adrian, "Listen, Boet, I'm going to shoot two animals close by as quickly as possible. They won't scent us with the south easter blowing towards us. After I shoot, you must aim well over their heads and try to ricochet your bullets off those rocks at the end of the valley. That might chase them back towards us."

"How the hell do you fire ricochets?"

"Just use your *Kop*, stupid! Right, are you ready? They're completely unaware of us."

Both boys shifted their bodies to find a comfortable position, released their safety catches and held their breaths as they took aim. Johan's first shot cracked and echoed round the valley. He swore under his breath, having missed, but reloaded rapidly and fired off two shots in quick succession. Adrian heard his grunts of satisfaction as he scored direct hits. The herd had now become panic-stricken. Most of the graceful, fawn-coloured antelope were sprinting towards the other end of the valley, their lyre-shaped horns laid back as they stretched into a full gallop. Others were giving the alarm signal by bounding, stiff-legged, high into the air, while flaring the white patch on their rumps. Adrian fired well above their heads towards the boulders at the far end of the valley, but the reports sounded little louder than those of a popgun. Johan then tried his luck and the echo of the powerful rifle confused the buck and the sprinting herd swung away and came back towards them.

This time Johan took his time and dropped three animals methodically. Adrian got in a lucky shot, wounding a mature ram. Johan turned his rifle on it and put it out of his misery. He then called a halt, proclaiming that six were enough.

They spent the next several hours bleeding the animals, gutting the carcasses and packing them on the mules for the long haul home. Johan was uneasy about returning through the kloof where leopards were known to range. The springbok carcasses would be too much of a temptation for them. Instead, they took the long way home around the north end of Renosterkop, arriving two days later; tired, filthy and proud of their success.

Maria supervised the skinning of the animals and the preparation of the biltong. The skinning was done with care to preserve the hides for floor mats, chair coverings, knapsacks and even clothing. The meat was removed from the bones and cut into strips before being marinated for two days in a mixture of vinegar, salt, brown sugar and roasted coriander seeds. Thereafter it was wind-dried on wires, suspended across the enclosed veranda. The final product was shaved into thin slices just before being eaten. It was relished as a delicacy and as hard tack on long journeys.

The promise of the early winter rains was not fulfilled. As the winter moved into spring the natural pasture began to dry out, the wheat crop failed and by mid-summer the flow in the irrigation canal to Maria's vegetable garden dwindled to a trickle.

Last year's wool clip had just covered the December mortgage payment, with a little to spare for essentials. Maria's concern for the future deepened with every passing week and her worries were aggravated by Johan's frequent absences from the farm. She knew that he met often with Boer soldiers from the north who mounted raids across the Cape frontier, but he remained secretive about his activities.

In fact, Johan had become a devoted member of a secret commando based in Calvinia that assisted the raiding guerrillas in sabotaging British Property. They were also active in suppressing any cooperation between the local Cape Coloured people and the British authorities. They were particularly harsh on a prominent member of the Coloured community, known as Abraham Essau.

Esau was a blacksmith who had enjoyed a reasonably good education at the hands of Wesleyan missionaries. He had successfully encouraged the Coloured people of the district to resist the tactics of raiding Boer commandos and to declare their loyalty to the Crown. This was done by various means including the singing of patriotic songs, which infuriated the Boers. The raiding Boers described Esau as the most poisonous Hottentot in Calvinia.

On January 10th, 1901 Johan saddled his favourite hackney, filled one of his saddlebags with cartridges and slung the Mauser over his shoulder. He reached Calvinia in time to welcome an Orange Free State commando, under the leadership of Commandant Charles Niewoudt. The commando had entered the town with the express purpose of teaching the Coloured people a "lesson."

The Coloureds put up some resistance at first but after several were shot and others beaten and jailed, the resistance soon dwindled to a token amount. Johan at first took part in some of these activities; motivated by revenge for the beating his brother had suffered at the hands of Coloured soldiers. As the beatings became more violent, his enthusiasm waned for the cause. He decided to abandon his comrades who were still supporting the raiding commando. He made his final break when a group of horsemen, chanting threats and insults rode into a group of farm labourers, lashing them with whips. He could feel how the mob hysteria surged through the crowd like a contagion and it frightened him.

At the first opportunity, he manoeuvred his mount to the back of the mob, turned the hackney sharply to the right and cantered away down a side street. At the next corner a small group of farm labourers armed with sticks and rocks ran into the street to attack him. His first impulse was to turn back but he was too close. He spurred the hackney into a full gallop, shouting threats at his attackers. The powerful horse carried him through the ambush but a stone, thrown by a tall muscular youth caught him a glancing blow on the head. The scalp wound bled freely over his clothes while he fled as fast as possible in the direction of the farm.

Maria and Adrian cleaned Johan's wound and even stitched it closed in an amateurish fashion. He remained in bed for several days, pale and mostly silent.

One afternoon Maria was sitting by his bedside, when he spoke to her haltingly, "Ma ... I'm terribly sorry to have given you so much anxiety. I'm not going back again. We must now try to save the farm. I'll help you all I can."

"That will not be easy, Boet. I'm just grateful the Lord has spared your life. I pray every day that this stupid war will soon be over."

About a month later the news reached them that Niewoudt had ordered twenty-five lashes for Esau, who had collapsed after the beating. Finally on February 5th he was placed in leg irons and dragged for a mile out of town, where he was shot. Maria and the two boys were appalled at this news.

Maria was filled with indignation when she turned to the boys and said, "These people are not our kind. I'm ashamed to call them fellow Afrikaners. How could your father sacrifice his life for these barbarians?"

Adrian looked aghast and Johan remained silent. The silence persisted awkwardly for several minutes until Hester climbed onto her mother's lap, sensing the tension and unhappiness pervading the room. The boys murmured their good nights and left the room quietly. Maria soon followed, taking Hester by the hand.

The war dragged on and with it a steady decline in the fortunes of the Nel family. The early victories of the Boers at Magersfontein, Colenso and Spionkop were soon reversed by the sheer power of the

British artillery, forcing the Boers to resort more and more to guerrilla tactics. Their excellent horsemanship, knowledge of the terrain and keen marksmanship equipped them admirably for this kind of warfare, and they successfully pulled off many daring raids. So much so, that the British eventually loaded many Boer women and children into open cattle trucks, sending them hundreds of miles to concentration camps to prevent them supporting the guerrillas.

Incredible as it may have seemed at the time, the ragtag Boer army of amateurs was tying up the largest expeditionary force ever to have left the shores of Britain. Maria's revulsion at the behaviour of Niewoudt's lynching of Esau became tempered when she read about conditions in these concentration camps, where thousands of women and children were dying in squalid conditions. The torching and destruction of hundreds of farms and the wholesale killing of sheep and cattle filled her with anger and dismay. She had few qualms, therefore, in welcoming a raiding Boer commando secretly to the farm much later in the year.

She had been given adequate warning and the whole family made preparations for the commando's overnight stay. The shearing shed was swept clean and filled with fresh straw. The kitchen produced heaps of fresh bread, while Maria roasted several legs of mutton and what seemed like cauldrons of roast potatoes.

The commando arrived at dusk and Maria soon realised that their leader was someone exceptional — the antithesis of Niewhoudt. He was carefully dressed in riding breeches, polished boots and a well-cut khaki tunic. He carried himself with assurance and dignity. His neatly trimmed goatee and piercing blue eyes spoke of authority and discipline. Not surprisingly, he had earned a reputation for arrogance and the nickname of Grey Steel. Nevertheless, he treated Maria with great courtesy, thanking her in advance for her help and offering his condolences for the loss of her husband.

The men were to sleep in the shearing shed but the leader was accommodated in the comfortable spare room. He took his time cleaning up at the washstand and then ate sparingly in the front room, while the men tackled their food boisterously in the kitchen and dining room.

Later that evening Maria took her children through to the front room to introduce them to the leader. He smiled warmly at Hester and shook hands politely with Johan, brushing off his fawning compliments with some impatience. The leader showed Adrian the text he was reading. It was by Virgil in the original Latin and he told Adrian about the exciting boat race that he had just finished reading.

He went on to encourage Adrian to study hard, saying, "Not only will it allow you to make more decisions for yourself and make you less dependent on those of others, but you will discover that there are few pleasures that can compete with those of the intellect. Besides, we Afrikaners will need many educated men when this war is over." His name was Jan Christiaan Smuts.

Not long after Smuts's visit, her attorney, Meneer du Toit summoned Maria, to Calvinia. As she expected, the situation was desperate. The bank was going to foreclose on the farm if the interest on the mortgage could not be met by next month.

"It's not the end of the world, Mrs Nel," Du Toit tried to reassure her. "I have a buyer for the farm at a price that will pay off the mortgage and allow enough over for you to live modestly for at least the next few years."

Maria glanced at Johan, who nodded his assent, and then she

replied, "If there is no other way out, you must go ahead." Adding bitterly, "We shall start our preparations to leave the farm and join the thousands of poor whites flocking to the towns and the cities, because of the evil Imperialists." She shook hands with Du Toit and almost ran from the office to hide the threatening flood of tears.

Maria's expectation of the worst had led her several months ago to write to her cousin Katherina who lived in the rural town of Worcester, some sixty miles east of Cape Town. Katie had replied to Maria, sympathising with her predicament, and telling her about a small cottage she had found in the Onderdorp, which could be rented for an apple and an onion. She would welcome Maria's family to Worcester and help them to settle down.

The next few weeks slipped by quickly with the many preparations required for their departure. Maria and Johan had agreed that they would load their best furniture and personal belongings on the large wagon, which the four hackneys could pull comfortably. Maria packed their most treasured possessions in old yellowwood chests. These were firmly secured in the centre of the wagon.

The evening before their departure they divided the reject furniture and clothes among the farm workers and their families. They said emotional good-byes to everyone but did not shake anybody's hand. Maria, however, found Griet alone in the kitchen and after a slight hesitation embraced her warmly and tearfully. It was a small gesture after sharing their lives for over twenty years, but it reached across centuries of prejudice and alienation and both women were deeply moved.

The same evening Maria insisted that they leave early the next morning to avoid the shame of trekking through Calvinia like poor whites, with all their goods and chattels on public view.

Her plan worked, but it was an exhausted little family that eventually found itself on the other side of the town, as the sun rose swiftly over the plain. The immense, cloudless sky dwarfed them as they slowly trekked across the wide expanse of arid veld, filled with anxiety about their future.

5

The cottage that Cousin Katherina had reserved for Maria was utterly without charm; a little square box set in a neglected garden in the unfashionable Onderdorp. To add insult to injury, some of the neighbours were Cape Coloureds. Maria greeted them all politely but avoided any close social contact with them.

Over the past three years she had worked hard at making the cottage habitable. She and the children had scraped and sanded down the pine floor boards and then polished them with wax until they glowed. She raided her savings to buy lime wash for the boys to paint the cottage inside and out. Johan cleared all the weeds from the front yard, while Maria pruned, mulched and watered the spindly rose trees. The back yard became Maria's proudest achievement. She and the children cleared out all the rubbish, pruned the neglected old fruit trees and created a productive vegetable and herb garden.

The boys shared a bedroom; Maria had her own small bedroom that Hester shared for dressing. Hester slept in a fold-down cot in the tiny front parlour, used almost exclusively for the dominee's periodic visits to bless the family and remind them of their financial obligations to the church. The small dining room became the centre for family life. The old yellowwood furniture was attractively enhanced by the polished flooring and Maria usually managed to have fresh flowers from the garden on the table. Here they took their meals and held evening prayers, but not until the children had completed their homework under the stern eye of Maria. There was no bathroom and only one cold water tap in the kitchen sink. The privy, a longdrop at the foot of the garden, smelled of Jeyes fluid. A galvanised water tank collected rain water from the corrugated iron roof. This was carefully husbanded and only used for the vegetable garden and for washing Maria's and Hester's hair.

Katherina had tried to help Maria cope with the shock of her impoverished circumstances, but her own family was also in difficulties. After the war ended, she urged Maria to approach the local magistrate for compensation for the loss of the thoroughbreds at the time Adrian was so badly beaten. Maria wrote a formal letter in her fine copperplate hand and waited patiently at the magistrate's offices to present it personally to him. She was repeatedly turned away by junior clerks but remained determined to meet the magistrate personally.

Eventually an appointment was made and the magistrate listened courteously while Maria read her request out aloud in very formal English. After she finished, the English-speaking magistrate enquired about the receipts she should have received from the British officer in question. On hearing that none was issued, he ended the interview with an abrupt few words of regret and, despite her protestations, led her firmly but politely from his office.

Maria walked briskly from the offices, her face burning with shame and anger in the realisation that she had been suspected of fraud. By the time she reached her cottage, however, she had regained her composure and promised herself to carry on determinedly for the sake of the children. They would, she prayed fervently, overcome the family's grinding poverty one day and set her free from her constant anxiety about the future.

Fortunately the children now enjoyed far better schooling than they had in Calvinia. Johan had completed three years of schooling, specially provided for young adults who had missed school because of the war. He also worked part time for a large grocery store, delivering groceries piled into a large basket on top of the handlebars of the firm's sturdy old bicycle.

Adrian had taken naturally to high school much like a likkewan sliding into a river. He had a part time job selling newspapers every afternoon on the busiest corner of the town. After selling his quota of newspapers, Adrian was given a free copy to take home. The whole family treasured it because of the acute shortage of reading material in their lives. Johan read the political news with disdain and described the Afrikaners, who were co-operating with the British, as "joiners" and "hendsoppers." Maria and Adrian were fascinated by world events and Maria would cluck in dismay after reading that thousands had died in an earthquake in San Francisco, or that the Japanese army had killed as many as 200,000 Russians in the previous year.

On Saturday mornings Adrian also worked at the stables of the transport company that had bought their hackneys shortly after they had arrived in Worcester. They paid him a small amount to groom the horses, clean their hooves and pitch fresh hay into the adjoining barn. The hackneys remembered him well, often whinnying and tossing their heads in greeting.

Growing up rapidly, Hester took obvious pride in helping her mother with the kitchen and garden chores. Her brothers both spoiled and teased her. She accepted it all in good humour until they made fun of her homemade gym skirt and blouse; this usually ended in temper tantrums and tears. Maria would then reward the instigator with several ringing cuffs about the ears.

By 1905 their memories of the war were beginning to fade and the family had almost come to terms with their lot, if somewhat grudgingly. Early in the New Year, Johan had learned that he had passed his examinations well and earned the coveted School Leaving Certificate. Maria arranged a special tea party and invited Katherina's family to help celebrate the event. Her best tea service was displayed on the dining table, decorated with fresh flowers. She had made a sponge cake, thinly sliced savoury sandwiches and sugar buns flavoured with aniseed, known as *Mosbolletjies*. Katherina contributed a fruit cake, rich with nuts and glacé fruit. These were all such unusual treats that an atmosphere of near reverence hung over the proceedings.

Katherina's husband, Francois, broke the ice by producing a bottle of sweet fortified wine and pouring a small glass for everyone. Even Hester received a tiny portion to taste. After rolling a mouthful of the aromatic wine over his tongue and licking his lips in appreciation, he turned to Johan. "So now, Johan, what are you going to do with all this learning? The whole family is counting on you. You won't be delivering groceries all your life, I hope?"

Johan smiled, "No, Uncle Frans, I'm not quite sure what to do yet. The Principal has given me a good testimonial and next week I'll start looking for work in earnest."

"Well, let's hope you'll be able to stay in Worcester." Francois said. "Maria needs you and, besides, where would we find another eighth man for our rugby team."

The wine soon loosened the stiffness of the occasion and flushed their smiling faces. Enthusiastic banter flowed around the table, reflecting the shared happiness of the two families.

True to his word Johan, armed with his certificate and testimonial, started the tiring and frustrating business of knocking on the doors of every business establishment in town. Before leaving each morning Maria and he worked on his shabby sports coat and flannels to give him a semblance of respectability. Even Adrian helped by polishing Johan's shoes and mending them with harness tools, borrowed from the stables.

After two weeks of job hunting in Worcester and the surrounding district Johan was becoming desperate. He decided to continue making deliveries for the grocer until something cropped up. One afternoon he was surprised to be told to deliver a small package personally to the manager of the local branch of the Standard Bank. The manager treated him courteously, amused by Johan's obvious surprise at the grandeur of his office and the dignified atmosphere of the bank.

Johan told Maria that evening about his impressions of the bank and how much he would like to work there. After much discussion they agreed he should approach the manager directly for a position at the bank and the next day they took special care in grooming him for his visit.

On arriving at the bank he asked to see the manager urgently. One of the clerks told him that was impossible without an appointment. By now Johan had developed into a tall muscular young man with an imposing presence, in spite of his shabby clothes. He moved closer to the clerk, held eye contact with him and said, "Listen here, *Snotneus,* this is an important matter and you would be wise to arrange an interview right away."

The clerk scuttled away and returned after a few minutes to invite Johan into the manager's office. The manager, Petrus Terblanche, had been appointed to Worcester because of his knowledge of farming, his effortless bilingualism and genial disposition. He could discuss banking matters intelligently with senior bankers in Cape Town and was equally at home mulling over farming problems with the local farmers. He was, however, essentially an Afrikaner and privately felt bitter about Britain's role in the recent war.

He greeted Johan in English, "Hullo, there. You were here yesterday, weren't you?"

"Yes, sir, you may remember I delivered a package to you." Johan came straight to the point. "My name is Johan Nel and I would like to speak to you about getting a job at your bank."

On hearing Johan's accent, Terblanche switched to Afrikaans, "Well now, that's quite a tall order. But, wait a bit, don't you play eighth man for the town's rugby team?"

"Yes, sir, we have an enthusiastic team."

"That's right. Now I remember, you scored an exciting try against the Robertson team. Well, well ... tell me a little about yourself, before we go any further."

Johan told him the story of his family's misfortunes, trying not to sound too rancorous about the British as he realised that the bank was controlled by the English establishment. He left his certificate and testimonial with Terblanche, who assured him he would look into the possibilities of employing him, but he should not get his hopes up too high.

For the next three weeks Johan and Maria waited anxiously each day for the post to arrive. Johan continued to deliver groceries as the family depended heavily on the few shillings he earned.

One morning while Johan was on his rounds the postman delivered an important looking envelope addressed to him. Maria carried it reverently to the dining room table, propped it up against a vase of

66

flowers and waited with increasing dread and excitement for Johan's return. He had hardly stowed his bicycle away when she rushed out to greet him and lead him to the letter. Johan sat down calmly, produced his pen knife, slit the envelope open carefully, "Calm down, Ma, you're making me nervous," he said.

"Hurry up, Boet; I'm dying to hear the news."

Johan unfolded the letter and read aloud. "Dear Sir, Further to our discussion of the 4th ultimo, we are pleased to offer you the position of learner clerk at the Worcester branch of this bank from March 1st, 1905, at a starting salary of thirty shillings per week. Please inform this office as soon as possible if you wish to accept this offer. Yours faithfully, P. Terblanche, Manager."

Maria turned away with her eyes streaming — her relief and gratitude were almost too much to bear. Johan rose from his chair, put his arm around his mother's shoulders and said, "Now we'll show the buggers." This was the very first time he had ever sworn in front of his mother.

For the next two years Johan worked hard to make a good impression at the bank, while Adrian continued to succeed at his studies. He was lucky during his senior years at high school to have an enthusiastic and competent schoolmaster, Anton de Wet, to teach him mathematics and English literature. Most teachers at the high school were Afrikaners. They gave their lessons only in English but always addressed the boys informally in Afrikaans. At some of the other schools if a pupil spoke Afrikaans, they were forced to wear a board around their necks with the word "Donkey" written on it. Fortunately, the Worcester school escaped this divisive practice. The teachers were highly conservative and took great pains to teach their subjects thoroughly. Discipline was harsh, a hard slap in the face or a painful caning on the backside were frequently meted out.

Anton de Wet was different; he sparkled with enthusiasm for his subjects and the gifted pupils responded to him. He had studied in Cape Town and had become sufficiently anglicised to develop a great love for the game of cricket. Adrian came under his spell, enjoyed his teaching, and even became adept at slow spin bowling.

Late one afternoon, after a disappointing cricket game in which the batsmen punished Adrian's bowling, he started to walk home past the ablution block, feeling somewhat depressed at his performance. The school yard was deserted and he was surprised to see a small group of boys from his class playing marbles under a large blue gum tree. Most of his class mates had long since outgrown marbles and he teased them lightly for playing such a childish game. The largest of the group, Frik Bezuidenhout, looked up angrily, "Bugger you, Engelsman. You can't talk. You've been sucking around De Wet, playing that moffie game cricket."

The hostility of their mood was palpable and Adrian decided to say nothing and walk on, but they all got up and started to follow him, taunting him with insults. Eventually they cornered him and dragged him back behind the ablution block, where two of the boys twisted his arms painfully behind his back while Frik punched him from the front, insulting him with every blow, "*Jou fokkin moffie, ons sal jou goed opdonder!*" And then the final insult, "You blerrie poor white!"

The final insult enraged Adrian. He no longer felt any fear or pain, twisted his body free and lashed out at Frik, shouting back insults almost hysterically. The adrenalin surged through him as he landed some telling blows, until suddenly, silence descended on the group. The Principal on one of his regular walks had surprised them.

The dishevelled and bloody boys stood with their heads bowed in an embarrassed circle while the Principal berated them. "You are no better than kaffirs, fighting like barbarians. You will all report to my office tomorrow morning after assembly. I can promise you, you will not sit down comfortably for many weeks after I have finished with you. Now, go home. Get away from here!"

The next morning the Principal did not bother to enquire about the circumstances surrounding the fight. He merely thrashed all the boys in turn and warned them of the consequences of further bad behaviour. Adrian upheld the universal code of honour among school-boys of never informing on your mates. He accepted the unfairness of his punishment as part of every day life — to be borne without squealing. Frik never worried him again. In some strange way their experience later drew them together and they often shared jokes and ideas about their future careers. Even Frik eventually began to blossom as a student under the tutelage of Anton de Wet.

Soon after the beginning of 1907 Maria turned forty two. Her prematurely grey hair had now become white; her slender figure was still erect and supple from all her gardening, housework and the long walks to and from the shops. The strain of the past decade, however, showed in the lines etched below her high cheekbones and around her eyes. Much to her grief, like many adults of her age, she suffered almost constant pain and embarrassment from her teeth. Katherina advised her to have them all extracted by one of the local doctors, who used ether as an anaesthetic. She balked at first, realising how terribly ashamed she would be at not being able to afford dentures. She even joked wryly about the Old Dutch proverb that poor people had to learn to chew hard bones - "How?" she asked, "In God's name, was that possible without teeth?" In the end the constant pain drove her to the doctor, accompanied by Katherina.

Katherina brought her home in a carriage but once inside the cottage she had to rush off to attend to her own family. Maria was nauseous from the ether and bleeding from the gums. It was in this state that Adrian and Hester found her when they returned from school. They cleaned her up, changed the bedding and made her as comfortable as possible. Maria was touched by their genuine sympathy and the deft way they performed all the unpleasant tasks, she required of them.

Johan returned late from work but did not enter his mother's bedroom. He stood in the doorway to enquire, "How goes it, Ma, is there anything I can do?"

Maria held her hand over her mouth and replied, "No, Boet, don't come in. I look an awful sight."

"Don't worry, Ma, at least the toothache has gone. We'll look after you." He then left to make sure the younger children were preparing the evening meal.

Johan had by now completed two years at the bank and he knew they were pleased with his work. Maria's strict attention to grammar and good literature had given him a sound knowledge of both languages. He wrote an excellent letter and had received several compliments from head office for his well-prepared reports. He also had a natural gift for working with figures and his popularity in sporting circles did not go unnoticed at the bank. He therefore felt confident about approaching the manager for a personal loan.

The manager greeted him cordially, "Morning, Mr Nel. What's on your mind?"

As usual Johan did not dither, "Mr Terblanche, I'm sorry to have to worry you, but I'm forced, through unfortunate circumstances, to ask you for a personal loan of twenty pounds."

Terblanche's forehead furrowed as he asked, "Whatever for? Don't we pay you enough? You know that the bank frowns on loans to its own staff, particularly to junior clerks."

"I realise that, sir, but it's for compassionate reasons. An uncle of mine has fallen on hard times and needs some help with funeral expenses."

Terblanche was about to interrogate his star employee further but could see that the young man was acutely embarrassed and had steeled himself for this interview.

"Twenty pounds, you say?"

"Yes, sir."

"Well, as long as you understand that this will be the last time, I will approve a loan. Off with you now."

Johan drew the money the same afternoon and slipped out to deposit it in his mother's post office savings account. That evening, after the younger children had gone to bed, he told her proudly that she could now afford to get her dentures from the local dentist. Maria clung to Johan, unable to find words to express her gratitude properly. Later in her own room, she knelt to say her prayers, thanking the Lord for her children, who demonstrated their love for her in so many different ways.

The winters in Worcester were generally not as severe as in Calvinia. During June and July the north-westers occasionally dusted the peaks of the Winterberge with snow, and cold winds swirled around the modest little cottages in the Onderdorp. On such days, Maria left the door to the dining room open and built a good coal fire in the kitchen stove. When Adrian returned from selling his newspapers on these days, he loved to sit in the dining room, revelling in the warmth while reading a crisp, fresh newspaper. The fragrance of aniseed, cinnamon and other spices used in his mother's baking added to his pleasure.

On one of these afternoons he was reading about someone called Mohandas Gandhi, who was organising a campaign of civil disobedience against a law that restricted Asian immigration, when his mother, weighed down with shopping bags, unexpectedly entered the house.

She immediately sat down next to him and asked, "You will never guess whom I saw today."

"Tell me, Ma."

"Your Principal and Mr Anton de Wet."

"Really?"

"Yes, *Hartjie,* and they had so many nice things to say about you, I hardly recognised you. They expect you to do very well in the School Leaving exams at the end of the year and asked me to start thinking about sending you to College next year — no matter what the cost."

"Really, Ma?"

Maria's excitement was infectious as she discussed all the possible ways of raising money for Adrian's studies and he responded with his usual enthusiasm. Eventually she calmed down sufficiently to ask him, "What would you like best to study, Boetie? Your teachers say you could become a fine artist."

"I think I would like to be a doctor, if that's possible."

"I thought that's what you'd say. Let's wait to hear Johan's advice."

The evening meal began with the family holding hands while

Johan said the grace. Maria had recently given him this duty as he was the major breadwinner and the elder son. Both she and Adrian kept quiet about their earlier discussion until evening prayers had been said. Maria was not sure how Johan would react to the news of Adrian's success. Would he be a little jealous, she wondered. She need not have worried. On hearing the news, Johan's face lit up with pride and pleasure at his Kleinboet's achievement. He congratulated him enthusiastically by thumping him on the back and tousling his hair.

After calm was restored, they discussed all the possible sources of loans for Adrian's studies. Embarrassed by all the chattering, he reminded them that he still had to write the exams and then left the room to go to bed. Johan and Maria finally agreed that the best plan would be to approach Maria's wealthy cousin, Nikolaas Nel of Constantia, for a long term loan so that Adrian could study medicine overseas. There were no medical schools in South Africa at that time. He would also be eligible for a scholarship to complete the pre-medical studies at the South African College in Cape Town.

Shortly after the family received the good news about Adrian's success at school, Johan developed a bad case of flu and remained at home for a few days. On one of these afternoons, a tall soberly dressed man knocked on the front door and Johan heard Maria greet him before showing him into the small parlour. Later she came to his room and told him to get dressed and join them in the parlour.

When he entered the room he could see that Maria was emotionally disturbed, twisting her handkerchief and biting back her tears. She turned to him slowly and introduced the stranger, "This is Mr Bresler, he is a schoolmaster at Malmesbury. He tells me that your father died in his arms at the Battle of Colenso."

At first Johan was stunned by the news, then he recovered quickly to grip Bresler's hand fiercely, "I am proud to meet you, sir," he said, and then continued hesitatingly, "Please tell us about how our father died. We know nothing. We don't even know where he was buried." Maria then withdrew to prepare refreshments while Bresler spoke at length about Dirk. A natural raconteur, he elaborated on Dirk's fine leadership on the long ride to Colenso, his bravery during the battle and how his comrades had respected and loved him. He also explained where Dirk had been buried alongside other Boer comrades in Bloemfontein. Johan listened wide-eyed and asked many questions about the famous battle at Colenso.

He also asked Bresler how he had fared during the rest of the war. To which Bresler replied, "About six months after Colenso, I was captured by the British and deported to the Island of St. Helena."

"That's where Napoleon was confined, not so?"

"Yes, and we suffered from the same malaise that plagued him."

"What was that?"

"Utter boredom. But we tried our best to keep up the spirits of the young Boertjies with concerts and sing-songs. I even started a school with the very few books we had ... not even pens to write with. But I could remember some algebra and geometry and, of course, history is my subject. I filled several note books from memory, using the pens the men had fashioned from scraps of wood and metal. I still have them."

Johan was intrigued and then asked Bresler how he saw the future of the Afrikaner volk. This set Bresler off on a long rambling description of how Afrikaners throughout South Africa were beginning to organize themselves into a Bond of Brothers, dedicated to restoring their freedom and independence from Britain.

74

"Yes," he concluded, "We shall be needing the help of our very best people; teachers, dominees, doctors, lawyers and even bankers. If we can't take revenge for the murder of thousands of our women-folk on the battle field, we will have to take it at the ballot box. One day, I'm sure, you will be called Johan."

Before Johan could reply, Maria returned with the refreshments and the conversation turned to more mundane matters. Maria was grateful to Bresler for the trouble he had taken to visit them and for his news about Dirk. But she reacted negatively to his intensely held political opinions and she was pleased to see him prepare to leave.

When Bresler prepared to leave, Johan thanked him profusely and made a note of his address. Bresler apologized for taking so long to contact them and told how difficult it had been to trace their whereabouts. As he left, he presented Johan with Dirk's worn leather saddle bag. Inside was his leather-bound bible, a note book, compass and a fine brass telescope. Johan asked Maria if he could keep the bible and note book. Later on he gave the saddle bag, compass and telescope to Adrian, who was grateful but also disturbed to get news of his father so unexpectedly.

With the end of the year fast approaching, Maria thought they could not delay a visit to Cousin Nikolaas in Constantia much longer. After a few days of procrastination she wrote a formal letter to Nikolaas, explaining their straitened circumstances as a result of the war, outlining Adrian's successes at school and his ambition to study medicine abroad. She tentatively asked if they might approach Nikolaas for a loan to launch Adrian on his career.

The reply came back surprisingly quickly. Yes, Maria and her son Adrian would be welcome to call on Nikolaas at his farm

Welgevallen on the afternoon of October 4th.

The usual frantic efforts to smarten up their Sunday-best clothes ensued. At one point, they even considered selling some furniture to buy Adrian some new shoes and a newer suit, until Johan slyly pointed out the advantages of appearing shabby when you were pleading for a loan. Johan planned the transport and route they should use to get to Nikolaas's farm. He paid for all the expenses but decided not to accompany them in order to save money.

On the morning of October 4th, Katherina's husband, Francois, arrived early with a horse and small carriage to take them to the railway station. The journey to Cape Town was only 50 miles as the crow flies, but it took almost three hours by train. On reaching Cape Town's main station, they waited anxiously for a branch line train to take them to the small seaside resort of Muizenberg. Adrian opened the windows wide and the combination of fresh sea air, the bright blue water and the colourful villas on the hillsides lifted their spirits.

"How *lekker* it must be to live here," Adrian enthused and Maria smiled her agreement. She wondered to herself how different her life could have been, had she not fallen in love with the quiet young racehorse breeder from Calvinia. Thoughts she seldom had time for in Worcester.

Francois had arranged for his brother, who owned a carriage in Muizenberg, to drive them back into the Constantia valley, where Nikolaas's farm was. After a long drive, during which the horses were rested twice, they arrived in front of the imposing Cape Dutch homestead on *Welgevallen*.

The homestead was laid out in the shape of an H. Its bright white-washed walls, thatched roof and elegant Dutch gable integrated harmoniously with the fresh green foliage of the surrounding oaks and vines. Maria and Adrian climbed several steps to the open veranda, that ran the length of the homestead. They knocked with more confidence than they felt on the double oak doors decorated with heavy brass handles. They did not wait long before a young Coloured maid, dressed in a black dress and white pinafore, showed them into a small sitting room, just off the main hall. Maria spoke to her in Afrikaans but she replied in English, spoken haltingly with a heavy Afrikaans accent. While they waited for Nikolaas, Maria took in her surroundings, marvelling at the beautiful Persian rugs on the highly polished tiled floor, the tasteful Dutch paintings and antique furniture. Adrian had never been in such a richly appointed room before and felt distinctly ill at ease.

Nikolaas did not keep them waiting long and on entering the room he ordered refreshments from the maid. They both rose to greet Nikolaas and as he shook hands with Maria, his childhood playmate, he was shocked to feel how hard and work-worn her hands had become, how she had aged and how ridiculously out of fashion her clothes were. He did not reveal any of these feelings. Instead, he greeted them cheerfully and exchanged family news and gossip with Maria while they enjoyed their tea and biscuits. He also told them about *Welgevallen* and his plans for developing new vineyards. The old vineyards on his farm dated back to the Napoleonic wars. In fact, they had produced some of the famous Constantia wine that Napoleon had enjoyed during his exile on the Island of St Helena. But modern wine making, he explained, required more subtle flavours and new grape varieties.

After tea Maria produced letters from Adrian's Principal and

Anton de Wet. Nikolaas read them carefully and then asked Adrian, "Why on earth do you want to become a doctor? You should rather study viticulture in France or Germany and then come back to help me on the farm."

Adrian smiled shyly and replied, "I'm not sure ... I think being a doctor would be interesting and something worthwhile to do. It's ... it's difficult to explain why ... it just appeals to me."

"Well, at least you're honest and not claiming a desire to save mankind."

Adrian blushed, feeling he had ruined his chances of making a good impression. But Nikolaas remained friendly and considerate while accompanying them back to the carriage. When they took their leave, Nikolaas promised to let them know as soon as possible if he could help them.

His reply arrived within two weeks. He first thanked them courteously for their visit and then went on to say that he would be willing to help Adrian start his medical career. If Adrian's final exam results were of sufficient distinction, Nikolaas would open a special loan account for him with Barclays Bank.

The remainder of the year passed quickly. Maria kept a close watch on Adrian's studies, exhorting him with her version of the well known Victorian adage, "The heights by great men reached and kept, were not obtained by sudden flight but they, while their companions slept, kept toiling onwards through the night." This would produce a wry smile from Adrian to please his mother and giggles from Hester, who knew how much it frustrated him.

Maria's ability to endure the constant anxiety, brought on by their abject poverty, depended on two important factors in her life —

her religion and the rare opportunities she had to indulge her love of natural beauty. Shortly after their visit to Nikolaas, Katherina invited them all to accompany her family on a camping trip to the nearby mountains. The weather was perfect, sunny blue skies, no south-easter to speak of, the soft air fragrant with the scents of the spring vegetation. Maria referred to these days as champagne days, even though she had only tasted champagne once in her life. She was transported by the spring flowers on the mountain slopes. The large, flamboyant proteas were the first to catch the eye, but the many varieties of heath-like Ericas with their small, exquisite flowers were no less impressive. They attracted the brilliantly coloured sunbirds that flickered shyly through the mountain shrubs, teasing the onlooker with their fleeting, jewel-like images.

They camped next to a small waterfall fed by a tea-coloured stream, where they soaked up the beauty of the surroundings and enjoyed the loving friendship between their two families. *Braaied/*barbecued lamb ribs, sandwiches and preserved fruit provided an unusual treat, complemented secretly by Francois's "medicinal" sherry.

As expected Adrian did well in his exams, obtaining two distinctions which earned him a scholarship to complete his pre-medical training at the South African College in Cape Town. This was a period of awakening for him. He met people from many different backgrounds, experienced his first innocent romance, read widely, learned ballroom dancing and for the first time enjoyed really good music. On his regular visits home, he tried to share these new experiences with his family, but he could already feel that they were drifting apart. This saddened him as his sense of loyalty to them was still as fierce as ever.

He enjoyed the College library and read voraciously, indulging his wide interests. Books about the recent war fascinated him and Conan Doyle's description of the Boers as, "Hard-bitten farmers with their ancient theology and inconveniently modern rifles," amused him. But Hobson's book on *The Causes and Effects of the Boer War* disturbed him; particularly the author's claim that the parasitic way of life of the Whites upon the subjugated Black people would eventually lead to the moral and physical degeneracy of the former, a phenomenon which develops in all slave-owning communities. Hobson was equally critical of the English settlers and this surprised Adrian. He considered buying a copy and sending it to Johan in the hope of tempering his radical political views, but later thought better of it.

Hester was nearing the end of her schooling and Johan had arranged for her to study nursing at the State's expense in Cape Town. She was excited at the prospect and felt she was following in Adrian's footsteps.

Finally, towards the end of August, 1909, the day for Adrian's departure from Cape Town on one of the Union Castle liners arrived. The day broke with a blustery south-easter whipping up white-caps in Table Bay harbour and producing a heavy cloud cover over Table Mountain.

The wind strengthened as the day wore on. By the time Adrian went on board, the south easter was buffeting the ship, scattering litter and raising dust along the quay. Adrian's family went on board with him to inspect his cabin before gathering in a small group on the quay next to the liner. Hester held several paper streamers connecting her to Adrian standing on a high upper deck.

Soon after the gang planks were removed, Adrian looked down on his little family and realised for the first time how odd and old fashioned they looked. Hester, dressed in a cast off school uniform was openly devastated at the thought of being parted from her Boet for so long. Maria's Victorian dress and bonnet were almost comical, had they not been so pathetic. Johan, tall and athletic, but cramped into a shiny, ill-fitting suit and tight collar, was trying to comfort the women under his protection. Adrian's heart was close to breaking as he realised he was feeling a mixture of both shame and pity for the people he most loved in this world. They had sacrificed everything for him and would soon be returning to their mean little house and shabby furniture.

Guiltily, he felt relief flood through him as the ship finally cast off, sounding three deep-throated blasts on its foghorn as it slowly edged out to sea beneath the majestic sweep of Table Mountain.

6

The city of Edinburgh in 1910 was by no stretch of the imagination an idyllic place in which to live. Nevertheless, it offered its citizens a great deal. In spite of the cold winds that whipped along Princes Street, the grey skies, mean tenements and the smog-laden atmosphere, the townspeople of Auld Reekie enjoyed its gracious sooty architecture, the cheerful pubs and elegant shops; as well as a rich cultural life with good music, bookstores and theatre.

Edinburgh University was the Scottish Oxbridge; it had earned an enviable international reputation, claiming scholastic giants such as David Hume and Adam Smith among its members. The reputation of its famous medical school, founded in 1685 by Sir Robert Sibbard, was at its peak and its graduates were sought after throughout the world. Adrian was well aware of his privileged education. He had fallen in love with his adopted city and took his studies seriously, but tempered with occasional treats in the concert halls and pubs. These were infrequent because of the smallness of his allowance from cousin Nikolaas.

His academic record during the past three years was above average without being exceptional, apart from anatomy in which he had excelled. Perhaps his exposure to the butchering of farm animals and wild game had given him a head start over the other students. The professor of anatomy thought otherwise. His experience had taught him that talented anatomists were rare birds indeed and he put their success down to their natural ability to form three-dimensional mental images of organs and organ systems. He also encouraged his students to study the functions of organs, not just their structure. "Anatomy, without physiology is a corpse, whereas physiology without anatomy is a ghost," was one of his favourite sayings.

Adrian's success in anatomy was not restricted to the theory; his dissections were used as models for the other students. This of course pleased him but, more importantly, it led to his appointment as a part-time demonstrator in the department, a position that paid a small stipend every quarter. This he sent home to Maria.

One particularly cold morning found Adrian in the company of three other students, wrapped in scarves and coats, making their way from their digs to the medical school. Conversation was desultory as they braced themselves against the bitter wind. Ian, a lawyer's son from Glasgow, commented that it was cold enough to freeze the balls off a brass monkey.

Adrian then asked him, "Where in the hell does that odd expression come from, or is it just another one of your vulgar metaphors?"

"It's an old naval expression," Ian replied, "The brass monkey was a brass shelf above the cannons that held the cannon balls. When it got really cold, the brass would contract differently from the cannon balls and the balls would roll off the shelf. Anyway, something like that."

"So, it's a polite remark then?" Adrian enquired teasingly, "Could I use it at the Dean's dinner table?"

"Try it and see, you dumb colonial."

The rest of the walk was mostly spent in silence but on entering the warm lecture theatre, their spirits revived and they took part in the general hubbub of pre-lecture gossip. The presence of a cadaver, laid out on a table in the centre of the room, did not disturb their bonhomie.

The professor of pathology entered the lecture theatre together with his assistant. The buzz of conversation died down immediately. He was a large man, dressed in a loose white coat, open in front, revealing a well-filled tartan waistcoat and gold watch chain. He swept his gaze around the steeply tiered seats of the theatre and began his lecture.

"Good morning, gentlemen." He ignored the two female students. "This morning I would like to discuss two absorbing cases, drawn from classical history. The first refers to the death of Alexander the Great, the second to those two biblical stalwarts, David and Goliath."

He had their attention and continued, "My first example concerns the mysterious death of one of history's most enigmatic characters, Alexander the Great. For the edification of our near-illiterate colonial students, I should perhaps first say a few words about Alexander." The South African and Australian students grinned at one another, some rolling their eyes in pretended disbelief.

"Alexander was the son of Philip II, the founder of the Macedonian Empire. He unified the warring Greek states after succeeding his father as king of Macedonia. In 334 BC he invaded the Persian Empire, leading over 35,000 warriors into battle. Within four years he had conquered most of the civilized world and at the age of 29 he defeated the Indian king, Porus. We are, however, more interested this morning in the cause of his death which occurred in Babylon in 323 BC, when he was only 33 years old.

"Historians inform us that Alexander drank heavily and even had a specially strong wine prepared for his predilection. We are also told that shortly before his death, his drinking took on heroic proportions. A final bout of drinking was followed by severe abdominal pain, lasting several days. Finally, he suffered from cold sweats, rigor and high fevers, eventually falling into a coma. His breathing slowed dramatically before he gave up the ghost.

"Unfortunately, we don't have his cadaver to dissect. So we must ponder on the little information we have and come up with an educated guess. Then," he added with a whimsical smile, "My colleague, Professor Robertson in the classics department can conclude his final chapter on Alexander's life.

"Well, there you have it. Would anyone hazard a guess about the cause of death?" The professor glanced up and down the tiers of seats but there were no volunteers.

He looked at the seating plan on his desk and chose a name, "Mr Carlyle, perhaps you would like to give us your opinion?"

The answer came in a broad Scots accent, "Ah dinnae ken for sure, professor, but I'm thinkin it might be pancreatitis. The same as our Edinburgh tramps develop on rotgut whisky."

"Yes, that might indeed be the case, although I wonder how Alexander would react to being compared to our notorious tramps. I assume your diagnosis is based largely on the severe abdominal pain associated with the excessive alcohol consumption. There is, however, more to this puzzle than a single symptom. Instead of staring blindly at a single symptom, we must always follow the sequence in which symptoms appear in order to draw a reasoned conclusion.

"If we do this, we note that an episode of heavy drinking of strong wine produced a rather sudden attack of severe abdominal pain. There are not many reliable references to previous complaints of chronic pain, which would be consistent with a diagnosis of pancreatitis. Moreover, we find that a few days after the first onset of pain, a fever sets in with attendant rigors, sweating and exhaustion. I, therefore, think that this is more typical of a perforated duodenal ulcer, which then caused leakage of the intestinal contents into the abdominal cavity, resulting in a severe infection, fever and a slow painful death.

"Can we now inform Professor Robertson of our conclusion so that he can finish his book and invite me out of gratitude to a posh dinner? Not really, because I must admit to withholding an important piece of evidence from you. Apparently, Alexander's body did not appear to decay until several days after his death. This could have been caused by a condition known as ascending paralysis; the person looks dead, lies absolutely still, but is in fact alive. This kind of paralysis occurs very rarely, but when it does, it is almost always associated with a perforated bowel caused by typhoid fever. On the other hand, he may have been pickled in alcohol! So, I'm afraid we don't yet have the final answer but we have given Professor Robertson at least something to chew on."

The professor then reviewed various symptoms associated with the pathology of the pituitary gland, which lies just beneath the brain. He gave special attention to a condition known as gigantism, which in his opinion resulted from a tumour that develops on the pituitary gland. These pituitary giants, the students learned, were frequently slow moving, clumsy people with little or no aggression. Unfortunately, because of their size, they were often persuaded to compete as heavyweight boxers. They were seldom successful, and he explained that he had collected statistics on how frequently they were killed in the ring, often with fairly modest blows. He then explained that he was developing an hypothesis that pituitary gigantism went hand in hand with tunnel vision and severe vulnerability to head injuries. "This," he concluded with obvious satisfaction, "was perhaps why

David was able to sneak up on Goliath and bring him down with a single slingshot with such ease." A bell rang deep within the building and the students filed out into a gloomy cold hall for a quick smoke before the next lecture.

Adrian sighed in resignation when the next lecturer entered the theatre. He was not only a distinguished physician, but also one of the leading botanists in Britain. He specialised in the study of medicinal plants and was responsible for teaching the students Materia Medica, a mixture of botany and pharmacology. The students found the subject utterly boring and loathed having to memorise the many Latin names of the medicinal plants. Attendance was poor and those who attended struggled to keep awake.

After almost an hour of boredom, he noticed from the wall clock that the end of the lecture was in sight and heard the professor raise his voice and move away from the lectern as he began to sum up.

"We have now concluded our preliminary review of the medicinal plants and the drugs that can be made from them, and I wonder what sort of impression I have left you with," he said. "Are you impressed with their potency and effectiveness? After all, you are now able to purge your patients rapidly and thoroughly, or bind their bowels like a rock; you can make their hearts beat faster or more slowly at will; you can reduce their fevers or make them sweat; you can render them unconscious; you can relieve their pain, make them euphoric or, if needs be, kill them with a few drops of harmless-looking liquid."

Adrian put down his pen to listen carefully as the professor continued, "You might well be impressed. We have come a long way from prescribing the moss scraped from the skull of a murderer hanged in chains, or the roots of plants dug from a graveyard during the dark of the moon. Nevertheless, do not be deceived by the variety or potency of our modern drugs, for there is not a single one capable of curing any disease. Yes, that may surprise you. But you should bear in mind that you, as physicians, can only relieve symptoms; only the surgeons are occasionally able to effect a permanent cure. If you realise this and retain your humility, you will be better doctors who concentrate on preventing disease and nursing your patients back to health by assisting nature to overcome the illness. As Voltaire said, 'The art of medicine consists of amusing the patient while nature cures the disease.' Thank you for your attendance." The students then began to move out to enjoy their lunch break.

Adrian and several of the men who shared digs with him walked home together, crouching against the cold wind. They were relieved to reach their old lodging house and take shelter from the cold. As they entered the small dining room, Adrian noticed that there was a letter for him on the old oak sideboard. He immediately recognised his mother's handwriting and stuffed the letter into his pocket as he sat down to lunch. The first course was barley soup — a grey glutinous sludge with an occasional hard barley kernel. This was followed by a plate of blood pudding, boiled potatoes and neeps. They filled up on some excellent fresh bread, which they smeared with dripping. This mess was washed down with strong sweet tea. During lunch the conversation turned to Professor O'Dowd's contention that morning that there was not a single drug in their huge pharmacological armamentarium that could cure any disease.

"It really is a depressing thought," said Ian, "Why the hell do I have to study all this muck if none of it is of any damn use?"

"To allow you to relieve symptoms, ox-head — a most important medical priority, or have you never suffered real pain, nausea or been racked by fever," replied Robert.

But Ian was not giving up. "Besides," he countered, "I don't believe he's right. Surely aspirin cures a fever and quinine can cure malaria."

"Sorry, old chap, both aspirin and quinine are merely for relieving symptoms. They aren't curing the underlying cause of the disease. The natural response of the body will do that if you help it along. But, I must say, you do raise an interesting point with quinine — perhaps we should challenge old slobber chops next time with that thought," said Robert.

Adrian left the table early, as he was keen to read his letter in the privacy of his room. After closing the door and lighting one of his precious cigarettes, he opened his mother's letter, written in her usual formal English. He read:

My Dear Adrian

I must apologise for not having written sooner, but I have been afraid to tell you that a crisis has arisen in our lives that is of the gravest concern to you.

A month ago we received a letter from Nikolaas explaining that he may lose his wine farm in Constantia because of the failure of several of his business enterprises in Cape Town. In short, he will not be able to extend any further credit to you to complete your studies at Edinburgh. In fact, he asked that you pay back your bank loan as soon as possible.

Shortly after receiving this news, Johan and I travelled to his farm to entreat Nikolaas to change his mind. Can you believe it; he would not even admit us to his house. We stood outside on the stoep like interlopers, ridiculed by that cheeky Coloured maid, whom you may remember. I have seldom felt so shamed.

Since then Johan has approached his bank manager for a loan and we both had a long talk to Mr Bezuidenhout. His son, Frik, is studying with you in Edinburgh. Mr Bezuidenhout has opened up bakeries in several surrounding towns and according to Johan is the wealthiest man in town. We asked him to consider standing security for a bank loan to you. He listened politely but then had the effrontery to turn us down with that old Shakespeare quote, "Neither a borrower, nor a lender be." He, who can hardly speak English, has no Dutch and only speaks a garbled Afrikaans. I was so annoyed and embarrassed.

Johan and I have racked our brains to find a solution but, as yet, have no idea where to turn. I am so sorry Boetie, what will you do now? If you have to return home, Johan says he will get you a position in the bank. If only I could get across the water, I would scrub floors in Edinburgh to pay for your studies.

We shall continue to pray for guidance from our Lord and, as always, ask Him to bless you and keep you.

As ever,

Your loving Mother

Johan added a short postscript in Afrikaans, saying they had tried everything, that he was profoundly sorry and hoped Adrian would be able somehow to *maak 'n plan.*

Adrian sat back on his bed, drawing heavily on his cigarette. At first he was too dumbfounded to react and merely stared at the wall, letting the letter fall from his fingers.

Eventually the reality of his situation penetrated his consciousness. He put on his overcoat and cap after deciding to go on one of his long walks around Edinburgh. Something he did quite frequently to clear his mind.

His route took him along Princes Street past the Scott Memorial. He then turned off to the ordered streets of the New Town, then through the Old Town towards the end of Princes Street. Here the splendid, towering castle dominates the famous street. The castle grounds were one of Adrian's favourite haunts. He had read enough Scottish history to appreciate the sense of history and excitement that the old grey walls and ramparts of the castle evoked in him.

After a steep climb he stopped to rest and look across the city. The early evening dusk was closing in and the light fog swirling below softened the lamp lights, turning the sky to a pale yellow with murky grey undertones. The walk had settled some of his anxiety and he promised himself that he would eventually find a way to complete his studies. He was determined not to return home empty handed. He strolled back to his digs where he joined his mates for high tea — sandwiches and strong tea. Occasionally the landlady provided a treat of boiled eggs and on high days and holidays, toasted scones and strawberry jam.

Adrian did not sleep well that night. He rose early with several clear objectives in mind. He would approach the Dean of the Medical School for financial help; either in the form of a scholarship or a loan. The professor of anatomy might be able to offer him a much larger stipend. His bank manager might help and then there was always his fellow student, Frik Bezuidenhout, with whom he had fought so violently at school in Worcester. They had become quite good friends and Adrian sometimes helped him with his studies, but they lived entirely different lives. Adrian had to eke out every penny, whereas Frik, or Fred as he now preferred to be called, wore tailor-made suits and spent freely on beer and cards. Adrian occasionally enjoyed Frik's largesse after helping him prepare for an exam, but he was too proud to accept it regularly.

Adrian had to walk miles across the city to reach all his possible mentors. The Dean, after making him wait for over two hours, was most solicitous, but explained that the country was almost on a war footing and the university's funds had been severely reduced. The Professor of anatomy went so far as to phone the Registrar and several other influential people at the university. He took Adrian to lunch at his club after failing to secure any help. The bank manager's secretary dismissed his request with an indulgent smile, marvelling at the young man's naivety. He too reminded him of the threat of war on the horizon; making unsecured personal loans a thing of the past.

Some year's ago a Scottish diamond magnate, thankful for the wealth he had accumulated in South Africa, presented the South African students in Edinburgh with a spacious villa to use as their club. It was a favourite meeting place for the wealthier students, where they could play cards, entertain girls, hold parties and celebrate special events, such as a Scottish rugby victory over England. They also staged rowdy boxing and wrestling matches in the large music room, much to the annoyance of the neighbours.

Adrian was dead tired from trudging across town and was now becoming increasingly desperate. He had paid the rent for his digs until the end of the month but after that he had almost nothing and nowhere to turn, except to Frik Bezuidenhout. He turned towards the club, a favourite haunt of Frik's.

He found Frik playing whist with three other students, shrouded in a fog of cigarette smoke. From Frik's anxious expression, Adrian concluded that the stakes were high so he waited quietly in the corner of the room for the game to finish.

His patience was eventually rewarded and Frik stopped on his way out to greet him in Afrikaans, "Hullo, you miserable bugger! Why are you looking so glum, lost your virginity or something worse?"

"Slow down, Frikkie. I want to talk to you. Let me buy you a beer down the road."

"You buying? That's a change. Let's go."

After they had taken several pulls on their pints of bitter, Adrian felt he could broach the subject, "Look here, mate, I'm in big trouble. My Ma has written to say my allowance has been cancelled and I have nowhere to turn."

"You're not serious. How did it happen, just like that?" Frik snapped his fingers.

"Yes, I'm afraid so," Adrian replied and then explained how he had spent the day and how everyone had failed him.

Frik listened quietly and then said, "Jesus, I'm sorry, man. But what the hell can I do to help you? My name's not Croesus."

"I thought you might write to your father and ask him to stand security for a loan in Worcester."

"Look, mate, you don't know my pa. He considers debt to be one of the cardinal sins . . . up there with murder, rape and fraud. He's a zealot, man. You can forget it right now." It had taken Adrian a great deal of will power to swallow his pride and bring up the subject. Now he had difficulty in hiding his feelings of disappointment and dejection.

Frik was looking at his watch and gulping down his beer. "Sorry, old man, but I'm already late for a rehearsal. Have to go . . . see you later," he called on his way out. Adrian reminded himself that Frik was an active member of an amateur dramatic society.

93

Adrian returned to his digs with a splitting headache. He missed high tea and fell into a deep sleep which lasted until early the next morning. He woke to an ice cold room and a single glance from his second-story window confirmed that rain was moving across the old city in swathes, turning the streets into torrents and making the drain pipes ring and gurgle with gushing rainwater. He put on two jerseys and a pair of thick woollen socks, knitted by Maria, then sat down at his small desk to write a letter home. He spent a long time composing it. He knew they would be offended if he merely brushed off his problems. On the other hand, he did not wish to worry them unduly. The letter was a model of compromise. He found a stamp and envelope and pocketed the letter on his way down to breakfast. This consisted of hot oatmeal porridge, a generous serving of milk, tea and toast. It was the same every morning and Adrian smiled when he recalled how a new South African student had once asked the landlady for bacon and eggs as a change from this monastic routine. She replied tartly, "Save your breath to cool your porridge, young fellah."

Adrian returned to his room to quietly smoke a cigarette while he pondered what to do next. He made his bed, tidied his desk and bookshelves, without coming up with any ideas. The rain was easing off and he decided to cut lectures today — there seemed little point in attending them. Instead, he decided to indulge in one of his favourite pastimes, a visit to the public library to read the leading newspapers. A habit that started as a schoolboy in Worcester.

The newspapers were full of the threat of war, with detailed descriptions of the weaponry and reserves available to Britain. He read these items with interest, but for pleasure turned to the stories on race horses, their trainers and breeders.

He skipped lunch, as he was sure Frik had gossiped about his predicament with the other students. Instead, he bought some fish and chips and huddled in a doorway to bolt down the greasy but tasty meal, wrapped in newspaper, and known by the students as fish and chips *á-la-journal*.

For the next several days Adrian moped around his digs, attended the occasional lecture and became increasingly anxious as the end of the month approached.

With only three days left, he had almost given up hope of finding a solution and decided to go on one of his long walks. He chose his normal route which took him past a small, army recruiting office. Some ten minutes later he reached a much larger one where a fairly long queue was forming. He stopped to read the posters that exhorted all able bodied men to perform their patriotic duty by joining the army — a plea that left him stone cold. But details of the pay, promotion possibilities and perks interested him greatly. After a few moments of hesitation, he asked himself, "What the hell, what have I got to lose?" And joined the queue.

It was almost an hour before Adrian came face to face with the two recruiting officers. One was a young lieutenant with a neat moustache; the other an NCO who assisted with the paper work.

After glancing at the form Adrian had filled in, the lieutenant looked carefully at Adrian and asked, "So you have almost three years of university training?"

"Yes, I'm in my third year of study."

"Why do you want to interrupt your studies to join the army?"

"It's quite simple, I'm broke," Adrian replied.

"I see you're originally from South Africa. This would account for your accent and your unusual surname."

Adrian remained silent, waiting for the officer to continue.

"Right now the medical corps is oversubscribed. Could I interest you in either the artillery or the cavalry? By the way, can you ride a horse?"

"Yes, I've ridden since I was a child," Adrian said.

"That's interesting but I'm going to assign you to the artillery. They need people who know a little science and maths." The officer said, and then added with a grin, "All you need in the cavalry is a backside of leather and lots of blind courage. Is that all right with you?"

"Yes, that seems fine. What do I do next?"

"Sergeant Johnson will give you another form to fill in and you must report tomorrow at oh-nine-hundred hours to the barracks at the end of Princes Street for your medical examination."

"Is that all?"

"Yes," the officer smiled and held out is hand, "Best of luck, old chap."

Adrian felt almost elated with relief and walked back to his digs to write a second letter home. He knew it would be another difficult one. His mother would be filled with anxiety about his safety and Johan would be furious to learn he was going to join the armed forces of perfidious Albion.

On entering his room, he found an envelope pinned to his pillow. He opened it to find three crisp five pound notes and a short note, "Pay me when you can. *Alles van die beste* — Frik."

Frik's generosity affected Adrian deeply and, after composing himself, he went downstairs to where the students were gathering for the evening meal. He found Frik at the centre of a group of Australians and waited for them to disperse before gripping his hand and thanking him warmly.

When Frik heard of his decision to join the army, he dashed into the dining room, rounding up Adrian's friends to give them the news. "Tonight," he cried, as he rallied them around him, "There's going to be high old time in the Jug and Thistle."

7

Adrian and his fellow rookies were herded into a special troop train on a windy, cold February morning. They were dressed in prickly, khaki serge; their caps and epaulettes still without insignia.

Adrian fought his way to a window seat from where he sat and watched the sergeants rounding up the stragglers amidst the banging of doors, shouts and shrill whistles. Eventually the green flag signalled the all clear and the crowded train lurched into life.

For most of the recruits this was the first long journey of their lives. Most had not even left home before. The feeling of freedom and excitement spilled over into a babble of voices, shouts and laughter as they stowed their kit bags and squeezed themselves into the narrow compartments. For many of them it was also the first time they had received a half-decent wage and their first pay packets were burning holes in their pockets. Adrian still had eight pounds left from Frik's generous loan and this, together with his pay gave him an unusual feeling of prosperity.

The train passed through several grimy towns and sooty slums; the detritus of the industrial revolution clearly in view.

Sometimes unspoilt countryside unfolded through the window. Even the wintry landscape lifted Adrian's spirits. The sight of rolling pastureland, stone walls, flocks of black faced sheep and thatched homes gave him much pleasure. He kept a keen eye open for horses and was rewarded by the sight of a team of Clydesdales pulling a decorated beer wagon. This prompted much waving and cheering from the troops, while Adrian wondered if this breed would be used to pull the artillery pieces. He hoped so, as he admired their strength and docility.

As they progressed southwards, the landscape took on a softer texture with chocolate brown soils, tall trees, blond stubble fields, neat haystacks and bright green pasture. After leaving a long tunnel they were almost blinded by a spell of bright sunshine, making the hoarfrost on a group of skeletal beech trees glitter like splintered glass. Adrian pointed it out to a companion who was puzzled by Adrian's enjoyment of such an ordinary sight.

Whenever the train stopped at a reasonably sized station, the men poured onto the platform to buy beer and snacks like fish and chips, tripe and trotters, or just a sticky bun with a mug of tea. Un-used to drinking, many rookies were suffering; the toilets were awash in vomit and urine. Tempers began to flare in the cramped compart-ments. These episodes were short-lived, either as a result of some good humoured banter or a stream of abuse from one of the sergeants, moving through the train and dealing out cracks with a swagger stick.

Adrian was relieved to leave the train early the following morn-ing to take a bus, that took him and a group of his mates to their base near Salisbury.

The base consisted of several imposing buildings, many tempo-rary sheds, a large parade ground and extensive park land used as a shooting range for medium and light artillery. Little time was wasted in issuing the recruits with their full kit and the insignia of the Royal Artillery - *Ubique Quo Fas et Gloria ducunt*/ Everywhere Whither Right and Glory Lead. Within a matter of hours they were square-bashing on the parade ground to the accompaniment of shouted com-mands and obscene insults from the drill sergeants. Discipline was brutal both on and off the parade ground and living conditions were monastic — plain nutritious food, almost no free time and constant badgering by the NCOs.

Late one afternoon, their drill sergeant fumed at them, "You are the biggest bunch of ninnies and spineless arseholes that I have ever come across. Let's see if you can at least run fast enough to get away from the enemy. Line up here and when I say 'Go!' you bloody well better run for your lives twice'round the parade ground, because the last three will run again — dja unnerstand, you brainless sons of whores?"

Adrian was reasonably fit and through a supreme effort at the end of the run came in second. After the last stragglers had limped home, the sergeant bellowed out, "I've changed me mind. The first three twits will run again."

It was a salutary lesson about the military mind and one that Adrian would never forget. He realised he had no option other than to keep his head down and perform his duties quietly and efficiently.

Eventually basic training came to an end and the men were assigned to larger groups for actual gunnery instruction. This involved advanced training in transporting the heavy guns, rapid loading, setting of gun sights and developing smooth teamwork under simulated attack.

Adrian enjoyed the excitement of these manoeuvres and the thrill of controlling and firing the powerful artillery pieces. The officer in charge of his unit soon noticed his competence, particularly with the horses. One morning when their unit was returning to base with four young percherons pulling a light howitzer, the lead gelding on the off side shied and began to plunge in its traces in a state of full panic. The young recruit, leading the horses, abandoned them and there was a real danger of the horses bolting with a careening cannon behind them. Adrian moved forward as though he were attending to some fractious mules on the farm. He grasped the bridle, reassuring the animal with the same soothing sounds and words he had learnt at his father's side.

That evening, the same officer examined Adrian's file and discovered that he had almost three years of university training; his record at the base was clean and even his drill sergeant had given him an above average rating. The officer scribbled a note, recommending Adrian for officer training and attached it to his file.

Adrian was unaware of this until he had completed the second phase of his training. The next day he was summoned to the adjutant's office, who told him that he had been selected for officer training. If he accepted, he would be transferred to a military base closer to London, where he would spend two months in intensive training as a cadet officer. Adrian was delighted and, forgetting military etiquette, embarrassed the adjutant by reaching across his desk to shake his hand and thank him effusively.

Officer training suited Adrian well. The barracks were far more comfortable than at Salisbury. He enjoyed the lectures on ballistics, map reading, simple physics and trigonometry. The discussions on military history and strategy intrigued him. But, more important in Adrian's eyes, weekend leave was more generous and he was getting to know some of the many pleasures afforded by London. His fellow cadets introduced him to the dance halls, several famous pubs and music halls. He also loved scrounging around the many bookstores, as he was still an avid reader.

One of Adrian's instructors at this time was Peter Simmonds, a tall spare man; pale skinned and blond. Although still young, he was already a major and responsible for teaching the cadets elementary physics. This was only a small part of his duties, which mainly involved research on the latest artillery technology and advising the British cabinet in this regard. He still enjoyed teaching the cadets and was always on the lookout for exceptional talent.

He spent much time explaining Newton's laws of motion to the cadets with some telling examples. "Newton," he would say, "has given us a simple explanation of how important speed or velocity is in determining the force with which a moving body will strike its target. His law states simply that this force can be determined by multiplying half the weight of the object with the square of its speed. Therefore, with just a small increase in speed, we can increase the force of impact dramatically. For example, a medieval soldier wielding a huge broad sword could smash it down with all his strength on the neck of his opponent without piercing the opponent's chain mail. Why? Because the speed of the blow is so slow. In contrast, a feather-light arrow fired at great speed from a long bow will develop sufficient force to easily pierce a suit of chain mail. No wonder then that we are trying to develop cannons that will hurl shells weighing a ton at the speed of sound. I hope I have made myself clear to everyone?"

Simmonds and Adrian were soon on a friendly footing and on two occasions he asked Adrian to give his lecture when he was called to London urgently. When this happened the cadets ragged him mercilessly, debagging him afterwards in the dormitory for good measure. He took it in good spirits, knowing they would be pleading for help when the tests came around.

The remainder of the course passed uneventfully. Adrian made friends with the librarian in the local village. She allowed him to borrow books and even guided his reading in an unobtrusive way. He enjoyed reading H. G. Wells and Thomas Hardy, but his mentor did not neglect the classics and he soon came under the spell of Cervantes and his literary masterpiece, *Don Quixote*. The story of this bumbling knight impressed him with its gentle irony; its wisdom, style and compassion. It may also have encouraged him to keep on tilting at windmills throughout his life.

But Adrian did not spend all his time at the base. He and his mates frequently went on a spree, visiting London's dance halls and pubs; constantly on the lookout for pretty girls with adventurous spirits. On one weekend after some heavy pub-crawling, a group of cadets persuaded Adrian to visit a brothel in Soho with them. They had to walk miles to reach the place and when they entered the grimy little hotel, Adrian's nerve failed him. He fled out the front door to the accompaniment of catcalls and ridicule from his mates and their frowzy companions.

Walking home alone, he slowly sobered up, grateful that he had not risked acquiring one of the frightening venereal diseases, dramatically illustrated in the pathology museum at his medical school. He grinned to himself at the recollection of his professor's quip about the radical treatment of syphilis with mercury injections — "One night with Venus leads to seven years with Mercury. Don't ever forget it!" But, at twenty-four Adrian was still a virgin and these thoughts were poor compensation for his enforced celibacy

During the last week of Adrian's training Peter Simmonds invited him for a drink in the officers' mess. Simmonds confided in him that he fully expected that Britain would be at war before the end of 1914. He also explained that the country was ill prepared and that their most urgent need was to train as many artillery units as quickly as possible.

He turned to Adrian, "This is where you come in, old chap. I've been watching you and I've gone through your records. I'm sure you would make an excellent instructor. You are far more use to us at present as a teacher than as," he hesitated, then smiled, "as cannon fodder."

"What would that mean?" Adrian asked, "Where would I be based and what would my duties be?"

"You would have to return to Salisbury and take charge of training a unit of field artillery. The adjutant will be in overall charge and the NCOs will be responsible for discipline and basic training. You will give the theoretical lectures and the more advanced gunnery training. Your leadership and ability to build excellent teamwork will be of crucial importance."

Adrian smiled, "Well, it seems like a soft option to me, compared to going to the front. How could I refuse?"

"As you know you can't refuse. But I wanted to talk to you before signing the orders."

They then chatted amiably about their respective universities. Peter explained how much he had enjoyed studying physics at the Cavendish laboratories at Cambridge. He hoped to return there after the war to do research on atomic structure. Peter eventually glanced at his watch. Adrian stood immediately and took his leave politely.

Adrian's return to the Salisbury base was very different from his first arrival as a rookie. He now had a small cubicle to himself, where he could keep his books and a suit of civilian clothes. The bed was reasonably comfortable; hot water in the showers and the officers' mess occasionally served passable nosh. On high days and holidays the regimental feasts were almost baronial.

His reading ranged from magazines and newspapers to the popular novels of the day. He had also developed a strong interest in military history. One particular evening when reading some Assyrian history, he read General Sennacherib's impressions of his rout of the Elamites in 691 BC and was badly shaken by the gory details:

*The commander-in-chief of the king of Elam, together with his nobles
. . . I cut their throats like sheep . . . My prancing steeds, trained to harness, plunged into their welling blood as into a river; the wheels of my battle chariots were bespattered with blood and filth. I filled the plain with the corpses of their warriors like herbage . . .*
The chariots with their horses, whose riders had been slain as they came into the fierce battle, so that they were loose by themselves; those horses kept going back and forth all over . . . As to the sheikhs of the Chaldaeans, panic from my onslaught overwhelmed them like a demon. They abandoned their tents and fled for their lives, crushing the corpses of their troops as they went . . . they passed scalding urine and voided their excrement in their chariots.

Needless to say, they took no prisoners.

The training programmes were a mixture of frustration and keen pleasure. To watch a gunnery team, that he had trained, working like clockwork together as the guns roared amid shouted commands and drifting clouds of cordite fumes was still a thrilling experience. On other days the stupidity of some of the recruits or the sheer laziness of others made him fume silently. He also experienced for the first time how a Cockney could address him as "Sir" and make it sound like a swear word.

Maria continued to write regularly to Adrian, giving him news of the family, some small-town gossip and the latest on national politics. South Africa was facing a general strike with serious political implications and Maria was kept up to date by Johan. Hester wrote short loving letters, exhorting him to be careful and to come home soon. Adrian's replies were irregular but carefully written to reassure the family about his safety and well being. Johan no longer wrote to him but Maria confided that she often caught him secretly reading Adrian's letters.

On June 28th, 1914 the heir to the Austrian throne, Archduke Francis Ferdinand was assassinated in Sarajevo and the shock was felt throughout Europe. On August 12th France and Britain declared war on Austria-Hungary and on August 19th a large British expeditionary force landed in France. Thus Europe embarked on a modern war that would eventually make the Napoleonic battles look like half-hearted skirmishes. Adrian read as much as he could find on these dramatic events and discussed them excitedly with his fellow officers.

The pressure on Adrian and his colleagues to speed up the training of competent fighting men increased by the week and their frustrations grew proportionately. They were forced to send units to France that were inadequately trained and woefully lacking in confidence.

One spring morning after months of this hard and exasperating routine Adrian was called into the commanding officer's quarters, where he was surprised to see Peter Simmonds and his adjutant sitting opposite the CO's desk.

The CO greeted him politely, "Good morning, Mr Nel. First of all I must congratulate you on your promotion to full lieutenant."

"Thank you, sir."

"You know these two gentlemen well, so I won't waste any more time with pleasantries and come straight to the point. A few days ago the War Office sent down orders that your training unit must be transferred *in toto* to France to strengthen the defense of a weak sector on the front. This is also in accordance with a new policy that training units should not be exempted from active duty."

Adrian glanced at his two fellow officers but they remained still.

"Mr Simmonds has been promoted to colonel," the CO went on, "And he will be your commanding officer in the field. Captain Ingles and you, Mr Nel, will assist him in every possible way to organise the transfer of your unit. I'm sure, like all good soldiers, you are keen to see some action at first hand and strike a blow against the filthy Bosche."

Adrian remained quiet. Fortunately Captain Ingles broke the awkward silence with suitable platitudes about the unit's readiness and their enthusiasm to do their duty. After a discussion of some details, the CO wished them well and the three visiting officers filed out of his office. The adjutant left immediately, while Peter and Adrian lingered on the gravel pathway to enjoy the warm sunshine and share a smoke.

"Well, colonel, this has come as a complete surprise. What has happened to your research position at the War Office?" asked Adrian.

"Please call me Peter when we're off duty. No, I'm not surprised. I had a *contretemps*, in fact a real bust up with the mandarins at the War Office about strategic policy for the Royal Artillery. Their thinking is still mired in the early nineteenth century. I lost my temper with them. This is their revenge — to send me to the front."

"I had no idea. I must say that it will be a relief to get away from this deadening routine but, quite frankly, I'm not sure how I'm going to handle the real thing."

"Yes, Adrian, our moment of truth is approaching. It's time to put away the chalk and blackboards to test ourselves."

The two men whose friendship had grown steadily over the past year strolled towards the officers' mess sharing their thoughts and fears. The one a patrician intellectual doing his duty, the other an Afrikaner son, swept along by random events and opportunities.

Preparations for the transfer of the unit went painfully slowly. Simmonds did not have the common touch to persuade quartermasters to part with scarce items. Ingles, the adjutant, was a little more successful by blatantly leaving bottles of whisky on a QM's desk before a difficult negotiation. The most successful of all, however, was Sergeant Major Buxton, a large barrel-chested Cockney, who supervised the stables and the care of all the horses. He secured the very best animals to accompany the unit to France.

Over the past year, Buxton and Adrian had come to respect one another. Adrian liked to visit the stables and often helped Buxton to treat sick or injured horses. Buxton admired Adrian's skill with horses and paid him the ultimate compliment by addressing him as Guv instead of Sir, when they were alone. The pungent aroma of the stables and nostalgic smell of dubboned leather and horse sweat made Adrian feel at home when he and Buxton took a break to smoke a couple of woodbines in the warm tack room. As their friendship matured into trust, Adrian would sometimes smuggle in a half jack of rum and they would enjoy a few clandestine tots amongst the carefully polished harness and large bottles of obscure veterinary remedies, favoured by Buxton.

Adrian's close friendship with Buxton contrasted sharply with his polite association with his brother officers. Although he was respected, many of them were professional soldiers and considered him a bit of an interloper. After a particularly pleasant social event which included dancing, Captain Ingles drew him aside and said, "Although you are only a temporary officer, Nel, you should know that it is not quite fitting for a gentleman to dance as expertly as you do." Simmonds, upon being told of this incident, found it hilarious.

Eventually, when all was ready for embarkation, orders were delivered from the War Office that a special parade would be held to bid the crack artillery unit *Bon Voyage*. The Prime Minister and several senior generals would motor down from London to review a full-dress parade with regimental colours and military band. Newsreel cameras would be there and journalists from all the major newspapers. The PM would make an important announcement about the progress of the war and the propaganda machine went into top gear.

In accordance with tradition, the parade had to be led by a mounted officer and the first choice fell on Colonel Simmonds, the new CO. Simmonds's horsemanship was, however, in question. Equestrianism was not part of the physics curriculum at Cambridge. The obvious second choice was to invite Adrian and he accepted the duty gladly.

He and Buxton took great care in selecting his mount. A safe selection would have been a large, handsome bay with a quiet rather dull temperament. Instead, they decided to take a chance and use a fiery young Arab, beautifully proportioned with a delicate head and strongly arching neck. In preparation for the parade, Adrian rode him for two hours each morning, speaking constantly to him and habituating him to his signals on the reins and from his knees and spurs.

The day of the parade was warm and sunny. The senior officers on the dais wished they had worn tropical kit, but soon forgot their discomfort as the parade approached the saluting base. The untiring efforts of the drill sergeants were rewarded by the perfect rhythm and stylish coordination of the marching ranks of smartly turned out soldiers. The regimental band was playing a stirring march as the sun glinted off the fixed bayonets and highlighted the unfurled colours.

Right out in front, Adrian's Arab was performing superbly, straining with arched neck at its martingale, dancing sideways and then high stepping until Adrian corrected it. The Arab was bursting with energy and the rider gave the subtle impression that he was only just able to control his mount.

Just before Adrian reached the dais, he moved the reins to his left hand to draw his sword. With a rigid right arm he first pointed the sword to the ground and then swept it upright in front of his cap as his head snapped to the right in the time-honoured salute to the senior officers. The Arab sensed the change in pressure on the reins and shied towards the dais. Adrian spoke to it; at first sharply and then softly, as it returned to its stylish forward gait and he returned the sword to its scabbard in a single practised movement. Sergeant Buxton watched all this proudly as he led a team of powerful percherons, drawing an artillery piece behind the marching troops. As the band reached the dais, the heavy guns on the far side of the parade ground began the rhythmic firing of a salute to the PM.

After the guns quietened down, a visiting general on the dais turned to Peter Simmonds, "I say, that young officer who led the parade rides remarkably well. He must be a Sandhurst man."

"No, sir, he is a young Boer from the Cape Province."

"Really? Quite extraordinary."

That evening over drinks, Adrian confided with a chuckle to Simmonds that while saluting the dais, he had almost felt patriotic. Something he would never have said to the other officers.

Although the preparations for the unit's transfer to France had been frustrating, the actual transfer went off efficiently. Within three weeks of embarking the unit had settled in to its position on the front line, immediately to the north of a French artillery emplacement. Peter Simmonds had placed his heavy artillery behind a low rise, out of sight of the enemy. The enemy lines lay to the east of a series of British trenches in a shallow valley.

Well behind the gun emplacements, the unit had erected several shelters for the horses, stores and some rough accommodation. On the brow of the rise, a well-fortified dugout served as the command post and the communication centre. The unit was still busy building a fortified emplacement for light howitzers well to the north of the command post.

Since arriving at the front, Adrian's anxiety and fear of the inevitable engagement with the enemy grew. He began to rely increasingly on alcohol to sustain his morale. He performed his duties like a robot, slept badly and ate only sporadically. In analysing his feelings and comparing them to the calm and almost jovial demeanour of the other officers, he attributed his dread to the fact that this was not really his war. He was near panic-stricken at the thought of being killed or worse, maimed, for a cause that meant so little to him. He even contemplated deserting and fleeing to South Africa but soon realised that would be impossible.

Fortunately their sector of the front remained fairly peaceful. At night the occasional magnesium flare would explode above No Man's Land, turning the landscape into a ghostly silver glare. From time to time flashes of artillery fire leapt along the horizon, followed by a series of rumbling explosions. On one afternoon a British Tommy enfiladed No Man's Land with almost continuous machine-gun fire.

Simmonds explained that he was destroying the vegetation which could serve as cover for the enemy. All this eroded Adrian's confidence and increased his anxiety and feeling of total alienation. He was only just able to hide his feelings and carry out routine duties.

The unit had not yet fired its guns in anger as headquarters still wanted to keep their presence in the sector a secret. But late one evening a German reconnaissance plane flew over their position and, in spite of heavy small arms fire, made a careful inspection of their position before flying off.

The next afternoon dozens of shells screamed overhead, exploding well behind the lines in abandoned farm land. Adrian and a small detail were busy completing the howitzer emplacement, well away from their heavy artillery. A light rain began to fall turning the emplacement into a quagmire. Adrian insisted on finishing the task. The hard physical work alongside his men partially suppressed the gnawing knot of fear inside him.

While they shovelled mud and helped Buxton drag the field pieces into position, they again heard the persistent whine of a small plane flying just below the cloud base. It was the same aircraft that had visited them yesterday. The Tommies immediately opened fire on the plane, which ignored them and continued to fly in increasingly wider circles around their position. Adrian knew it was assessing the damage inflicted by the recent barrage and would soon report back to base to shorten the range. They could expect the next salvo to be much closer. His fear turned his stomach to jelly and began to paralyse his limbs, as if he was experiencing a nightmare. The field telephone rang in the adjacent dugout and he stumbled through the mud to answer it.

It was Simmonds, "Adrian, Jerry has found us and we can expect an attack shortly. I have orders to fire thirty salvos immediately at the estimated position of their green sector artillery. I shall direct the fire and the warrant officers will command the guns. I want you to stay with the howitzers and take orders from the infantry. Captain Morrison may need your help in repelling an attack on our trenches. Is that clear?"

"Yes, sir." Adrian mumbled and returned to ready his group for the attack. His arms and legs felt like lead and he had to force himself to speak coherently to the men. No one seemed to notice his predicament except Buxton who drew him aside behind two large horses and produced a hip flask of rum from his pocket. He watched Adrian take a few gulps before cautioning him, "Slow down, guv, we still have to shoot straight when we see the whites of their eyes."

The large imposing presence of Buxton and the warmth of the fiery rum in his gullet took the sharp edge off Adrian's fear. He organised the sighting of the howitzers and the unpacking of the ammunition. Before he was able to sit down for a smoke, the field telephone suddenly rang.

It was Simmonds; "Firing will commence within three minutes. Good luck, old man."

"Take care of yourself, Peter."

Suddenly their own heavy artillery thundered into life, electrifying them all. Confidence flooded through the ranks and both officers and men cheered with pride and relief. This was what they had trained so hard and long for.

The feeling was however short lived. Four minutes later, incoming shells tore into their heavy gun emplacements, destroying four big guns and killing forty men instantly. Limbs were torn off, bodies eviscerated and the recent calm discipline was replaced by screaming bloody chaos as a second salvo thudded home.

The howitzer fortifications were eight hundred yards from the heavy artillery. When the enemy barrage struck, the blast wave knocked Adrian off his feet. He landed on his back at the bottom of a muddy trench, struggling for breath as the fall had winded him badly. When his breathing became easier, he realised he was completely soiled; he lay quietly, frightened, embarrassed and angry.

After a time he recovered sufficiently to get up and inspect the damage. All the men had survived. Everyone was covered in mud from the recent excavations and his appearance would not be noticed. He climbed out of the trench and for the first time saw the chaos surrounding the big guns. He realised he had to pull himself together if he were going to be of any help. He put a warrant officer in charge of the howitzers, directing him to respond to any requests from the infantry captain. He then ran across to the command post and to his horror discovered that it had been destroyed by a direct hit.

Captain Ingles had somehow survived and was directing the removal of the wounded to the small dressing station near the quartermaster's store. Adrian climbed down into the command dugout dreading what he would find. As he had expected, everything had been destroyed and Peter Simmonds lay in an awkward sprawl against one of the walls. Adrian moved his body to a more natural position and in so doing, his experienced hands could feel that the explosion had shattered almost every bone in Peter's body. His body looked and felt like that of a rag doll. His pale, aristocratic features were unharmed and Adrian closed his eyes gently before turning away to weep like a child.

Soon after, Captain Ingles found Adrian and shouted down to him, "Get a grip on yourself, Nel. We need you up here urgently."

Ingles ordered Adrian to clean himself up and to help with the treatment of the wounded. The dressing station, manned by a half dozen medical orderlies, was a shambles. Bodies lay everywhere, horrendous gaping wounds defied description, while the screaming and moaning of the wounded unnerved the inexperienced orderlies.

Adrian felt strangely calm. It was as if his fear had been expunged by some sort of catharsis. He organised the orderlies into teams and got stuck in himself, stanching haemorrhages, applying dressings and roughly stitching wounds closed. His knowledge of anatomy stood him in good stead as he straightened limbs, set them in splints and searched for large blood vessels, bleeding between lacerated muscles.

Shortly after Adrian had restored some order to the dressing station a salvo of enemy shells screamed overhead, exploding behind them. He realised that the enemy was bracketing their target and that they could expect another series of direct hits soon. What he did not know was that the adjoining French artillery unit would soon be responding to an urgent request from their HQ to lay down a broad barrage behind the enemy lines. They were an elite unit and as their thundering salvos began, Adrian could feel his confidence returning while he laboured in the dressing station, covered in blood and muck.

Around midnight, a convoy of ambulances arrived to evacuate the wounded. Two surgeons, with fresh supplies, attended to the men who were in extremis. Horse carriages were being loaded with the dead, apart from Simmonds. His body was transported in a special ambulance to a major command post well behind the lines.

No sooner had Adrian sat down to rest after the surgeons arrived, when a stray shell exploded directly on the howitzer emplacement, killing eight men, beheading three of them and destroying half the guns. This news was the final straw for Adrian. He refused to carry on and collapsed, totally exhausted, outside the dressing station. Later on Ingles fetched a blanket and threw it over him.

After all the dead and wounded had been evacuated, the remainder of the unit worked aimlessly at clearing up the damage, but it soon became clear to HQ that the unit was no longer functional. Arrangements were made to return them to Britain for eventual posting to new units. Simmonds was awarded the military cross posthumously and Ingles the Distinguished Service Order. Adrian, Buxton and Ingles received orders to return to Salisbury to resume training duties. The officers were given ten days furlough.

Adrian spent his furlough in an almost constant state of drunkenness in Paris. On his very first night in that city he lost his virginity in a brothel and celebrated the fact by a repeat performance every subsequent night of his leave. After a week of debauchery he cleaned himself up, shaved carefully, dressed in his best uniform and made his way shakily back to Britain, his mind still numb with shock.

Life back at the training base near Salisbury was at first unreal for Adrian. He had become cynical and withdrawn. The training exercises seemed like pathetic games after the reality of war, while the political propaganda sickened him with its deceit. But he had no choice other than to discipline himself to carry out his duties efficiently and respectfully. He missed Simmonds's empathy and sarcastic wit, not to speak of his fine intellect. Ingles's attitude towards him had changed completely. Whenever he met Adrian in the corridors or on footpaths, he would shake hands warmly, holding both of Adrian's hands, without saying anything.

Adrian found solace in the occasional drunken spree in London, a companionable drink with Buxton in the tack room and in long hard gallops in the adjoining parkland on one of Buxton's choice mounts. And then there was the rare treat of a concert or the visit of an eminent musician to the base.

Adrian's correspondence with his South African family was erratic. He never mentioned his ghastly experiences in France. Instead, he wrote about the books he was reading, the course of the war and his hopes of returning to his medical studies in Edinburgh. Maria's regular letters were predictable, expressing her fears about his safety, how to keep warm and eat properly. One item of her family news that amused Adrian was that Johan had begun to pray for Adrian's safety at evening prayers. Before his transfer to France, he would not even mention his name.

Because of the strict routine at the training base, life slowly became bearable for Adrian. He made new friends among his fellow-officers. A young war widow, Priscilla, from the nearby village shared a friendship with him without either of them becoming deeply involved. She did not wish to become emotionally attached to a soldier again. They went dancing together, shared drinks at the local pub, held hands on the way home and concluded the evening with a hug and a chaste kiss.

Adrian's interest in his medical studies became rekindled. He bought several textbooks in London and spent many an evening browsing through them. He also studied Buxton's elementary texts on equine anatomy and together they often performed minor surgery on the injured horses.

Time passed quickly and not too unpleasantly through the winter of 1915/16. During the late spring of 1916 rumours began to circulate that preparations were under way to force a break-through on the western front, that was literally mired in stalemate. The big-wigs were planning a "big show". Adrian paid little attention to these rumours until late May, when all the officers at the base were called to a special meeting at the mess. The CO was in dress uniform when he entered the mess. He asked everyone to sit down and then began his address.

"Gentlemen, you may be surprised at being summoned at this hour, but you will also be aware of the rumours of an impending major attack that is being planned. I'm not sure if the War Office circulated these rumours to confuse us or the Germans. Whatever the case, this uncertainty has made it very difficult to make long term training plans at this base. At last, however, we have received a firm directive from HQ."

He now had everyone's rigid attention and proceeded, "Training operations at this base will be temporarily cut in half and about half of our more experienced officers and men will be transferred to the front so that their expertise can be used for what is now referred to as a special operation. Within a week your individual orders will arrive. Those who are going to be shipped out will have to leave on very short notice — no furlough will be granted. So say your goodbyes and get your gear together in case you are called.

"I must also ask you to keep your orders strictly secret — even if you have heard that Berlin cab drivers are taking bets on when the Big Push will occur. I wish you all well and Godspeed to those who are called up. Thank you."

The CO turned smartly on his heel and walked quickly from the mess, leaving a lively buzz of conversation behind him. Adrian left almost immediately for his cubicle, where he sat on his bed and quietly smoked a cigarette. He was instinctively convinced that his name had been drawn for active service on the front and the familiar gnawing fear was returning. This time it did not leave him paralysed with fear. He started to plan what to pack.

The following week orders were delivered to several officers. Adrian and Ingles learned that they would be assigned to the same artillery unit and that Buxton would accompany them.

Their long journey to the front was without incident and after only a few weeks they were fully integrated into their new unit. Their new posting was quite different from their previous experience at the front. Adrian noticed that the unit was much larger and the emplacements and dugouts far better fortified. The trenches had been occupied for months on end. The surrounding terrain, pockmarked by shell holes, had been grotesquely deformed. The trenches were filthy and rat-infested with macabre reminders of recent dismembering casualties from accurate mortar fire. Morale was low among the Tommies but there was also a feeling of desperation to break out of this hellhole, even if it meant throwing oneself into the cannon's mouth.

Adrian's dread did not return as acutely as before. He never conquered it completely, particularly when required to move about in the open. He forced himself to adopt a fatalistic attitude and his Calvinistic upbringing probably reinforced this attitude and helped to soften the dread with which he woke each morning.

By June 20th the plan of attack had been almost finalised, although senior generals were still bickering about important details. The main attack under the command of Lieutenant-General Rawlinson was to take place on a ten-mile front between Montauben and the River Ancre. Rawlinson had nine divisions under his command.

Officers in the Royal Artillery, including Adrian, had been intensively prepared for the attack. The artillery was to play a key role in the overall strategy. Rawlinson hoped that a constant heavy barrage of shelling would not only destroy the German trenches and machine gun emplacements, but also blast a pathway through the barbed wire defences; allowing the infantry to force their way through the German lines to deal a fatal blow to the enemy.

The first major barrage began at dawn on June 24th. The constant roar of over a thousand guns could be heard far across the English Channel. During the following week over 1.5 million shells were fired.

Throughout the initial barrage Adrian sat at a trestle table in the deep command dugout, frantically calculating fuse and gun settings for the gunnery officers, poring over their large-scale topographical maps. The dugout was heavily sandbagged and Adrian felt reasonably safe and confident in the security of this sanctuary. Above them all hell was breaking loose: shouted commands, the thunder of the guns and the acrid fumes of spent explosives dominated everything.

Heavy clouds moved into the area and light drizzle began to fall, preventing the artillery from assessing the effectiveness of their bombardment. Reconnaissance aircraft were grounded and hardly any intelligence leaked back to the command posts. Unknown to the commanding officers, the barrage had done comparatively little damage. Many of the German emplacements and dugouts had been constructed with steel and concrete and above all, with Teutonic thoroughness. The worst disappointment, which would only be realised much later, was that the shrapnel-spewing shells had failed to effectively cut down the enemy's barbed wire defences. Apparently the fuses had not been correctly set.

As soon as the Allied guns fell silent, the Germans emerged from their cover and hurried back to man their machine gun emplacements and to defend their trenches. At the same time, over sixty thousand British infantrymen, overloaded with ridiculously large packs, were ordered over the top to attack the German lines head on. Whole ranks of advancing infantrymen were scythed down by the enfilading German machine guns. The overloaded Tommies struggled pathetically to move through narrow gaps in the German barbed wire lines, presenting sitting targets to the enemy. They were cut down in their thousands by the vicious small arms fire.

Meanwhile the German artillery had reorganised itself and had started to lob howitzer shells into No Man's Land. This decimated the second wave of infantrymen moving up to reinforce the first wave. By midday British casualties exceeded 50,000 and the enemy had regained sufficient confidence to start a counter attack across a wide sector.

Some eight miles east of the German trenches, a German artillery officer, a successful engineer in civilian life, sat in a reinforced dugout with his aids. Behind him a huge 16.5 inch cannon, nicknamed *Dicke Bertha* / Big Bertha, rested on its own railway carriage. A team of over sixty men served the gun. They were on red alert waiting eagerly for their Captain's orders.

The Captain's field telephone shrilled and he picked it up instantly, *"Hauptmann Wehner hier."*

"Good morning, Wehner, I want you to consult your map of the yellow sector."

"In front of me, *Herr Oberst*."

"We suspect that the most accurate artillery fire from the enemy is emanating from this sector at coordinates B:14. Do you have it?"

After a short pause, "I have marked it, *Herr Oberst.*"

"Very well. We want you to fire three rounds into this target as soon as you are ready. The spread should be three hundred metres apart and the fuses set for maximum shrapnel dispersion. Is that quite clear?

"Quite clear, *Herr Oberst.* "

The captain immediately began his calculations, ordering his senior aid to check his results line by line. As soon as they were finished, the necessary orders went down the chain of command and the team of gunners sprang to their duties. The teamwork was a model of precision and efficiency.

After the Allied barrage had stopped, Adrian moved up to an observation dugout, where he and his fellow gunners could watch the progress of the attack through fortified slits in the concrete. They soon became aware that a disaster was developing. The infantrymen were being decimated as they stumbled forward, weighed down by their heavy packs. Even worse, it appeared as if their heavy barrage had done minimal damage to the enemy's fortifications. The machine gun emplacements were spitting out wave after wave of deadly fire and it was obvious to the artillery officers that a German counter attack was imminent.

At this juncture, Captain Ingles entered the dugout with the news that they had lost telephone contact with the mortar battery in the British trenches. The mortars had been ordered to remain silent during the offensive, but were now urgently required to plaster the German trenches to fend off the expected counter attack.

Ingles looked around the dugout, "We need someone to make

his way to the mortars and start a steady bombardment of the Jerry trenches between Red Four and Red Twelve; any volunteers? It's worth at least a DSO."

Before anyone could respond, his eyes met Adrian's, "Lieutenant Nel, you're our expert on mortar gunnery; I think you should accept this duty. There's absolutely no time to be wasted — best of luck, old man!"

Adrian did not reply. He put on a steel helmet and crawled out of the dugout in a state of controlled fear. His heart was racing in panic but adrenalin kept him focused on his duty,

He was running in a crouched position halfway towards the mortar battery when Captain Wehner's first Big Bertha shell exploded some three hundred yards away. The shock wave knocked him flat and deafened him completely. After a few minutes, he realised he had been hit — he felt no pain, only a sense of heat and numbness was spreading below his right shoulder blade. He could feel blood beginning to pool in the small of his back. He tried to move but felt faint and had difficulty breathing. He heard whistles blowing and guns firing in the distance. Just before passing out he buried his face in the soil, in much the same way as when the Coloured soldiers had flogged him near to death on the Calvinia farm.

Ingles personally rescued Adrian from further harm. He and a brother officer rolled him onto a stretcher and under sporadic, dangerous fire carried him to the dressing station.

Before they reached the safety of the dressing station they passed a team of Belgian horses, led by Buxton. He immediately recognised Adrian's limp figure, abandoned the horses and rushed over to grab Adrian's arm, "For Chrissake, guv, don't give up now." Tears began to stream down his burly face as he smacked his fist repeatedly into his palm.

Ingles, barely able to control his own grief, turned to Buxton, "Control yourself, man, you're making a spectacle of yourself in front of the men."

When the day ended, half of the attacking force of 120,000 troops became casualties, of whom at least 20,000 were killed outright. It would be known as the Battle of the Somme and, like Colenso, would go down in history as a major military debacle.

8

As Ingles entered the dressing station carrying Adrian, he immediately used his seniority to commandeer a surgeon to treat Adrian's haemorrhaging wound before leaving for his duties. The surgeon packed the wound with swabs and bound it tightly. It was all he could do under the chaotic conditions. Luckily, a convoy of ambulances and wagons had assembled to evacuate the wounded to a better-equipped station, well behind the lines.

By the time Adrian reached the field hospital he was semi-conscious from loss of blood. The examining physician found that his right lung had collapsed, due to pneumothorax. He was in grave danger of dying and required urgent surgery.

The field hospital was overwhelmed with casualties and the best the physician could do was to order a nurse to try to get fluids into the patient. The nurse persuaded a passing medical orderly to insert a naso-gastric tube through one of Adrian's nostrils into his stomach. She then patiently fed him dilute salt solution through the tube until she guessed that he was fully hydrated.

As soon as the Allies realised that they had a major disaster on their hands, their efficient organisation behind the lines jumped into action. They diverted ambulances and special trains to transfer the wounded to nearby hospitals and a hospital ship waited at Calais to evacuate the worst casualties to Britain. Because of a series of fortunate coincidences, they transferred Adrian with minimum delay to a fast hospital train bound for Calais. Here, he was one of the first patients to arrive in the surgical ward on the ship.

Captain Holborn, in private life a successful surgeon at Guys hospital in London, called the orderlies to bring his first patient who was Adrian. In spite of the crisis and the urgings of the chief surgeon, Holborn's high-minded attitude to his surgery was so disciplined and ingrained, he was incapable of rushing through an operation.

He examined Adrian carefully, palpating his wound, taking his pulse and listening to his heart and respiration. The patient was semiconscious during the examination, but cried out in pain as his shrapnel wound was examined.

Holborn then turned to his assistant, "This fellow is in a bad way; he has lost a lot of blood, his one lung has collapsed and I suspect there is a large dirty piece of shrapnel lodged close to his lung. But exactly where, I don't know. I can't operate blindly; he would probably die from loss of blood if I did. Wheel him to x-ray and bring in the next patient."

The x-ray confirmed that a jagged piece of shrapnel had smashed through two of Adrian's ribs and the adjoining intercostal muscles, before lacerating his right lung.

"Well, let's get on with it," Holborn said to his assistant, as they turned him over and carefully removed his dressing. The sight of the whipping scars on his back prompted him to tease his assistant; "This chap must have been with you at Eton? At Marlborough our masters could aim straight for the backside. Scalpel please, nurse."

With a minimum of bleeding, Holborn's skilful hands parted the various tissue layers to reach and remove the shrapnel. He then closed the surgical wound and cleaned up the entry wound, clearing away necrotic tissue before, finally inserting a chest drain to heal the collapsed lung.

Adrian passed the rest of the voyage in a haze of nausea, pain and occasional mild euphoria from the morphine injections. He was only vaguely aware of the stretcher-bearers who took him off the ship at Southhampton.

Special trains waited at Southampton to convey the wounded to various London hospitals. They delivered Adrian to a small nursing home near King's Cross, recently converted into a military hospital. A military doctor, Captain Henderson, carried out ward rounds there twice daily, but the reputation of this well-run establishment was largely due to the devoted efforts of a Sister Thompson and her enthusiastic volunteers. She was still young and attractive; characteristics much appreciated by her patients who responded to her feminine compassion and encouraging homilies to brave their pain and, in many cases, to overcome deep depression from their mutilating wounds. Not an easy task in this grim environment, pervaded by the moans and cries of badly wounded men, the odour of body wastes, ether and disinfectants.

Her welcome to Adrian did not seem to touch him. He did not even respond to her with a flicker of his eyelids, remaining in a state of deep autistic depression. He refused to eat, spoke to no one and wet his bedclothes regularly. By lifting him into almost a sitting position, the volunteer aids were able to spoon a little thin soup into him. It was hard messy work and tried everyone's patience. Eventually they fitted him with a naso-gastric tube and fed him via this route.

Three weeks after his arrival he started to run a fever. Captain Henderson found that an abscess had formed in the old entry wound. He decided to drain it and sedated him heavily before the procedure.

127

The abscess drained well and the wound eventually began to heal, but there was no change in his autism and depression. Sister Thompson had read about a condition, recently described as shell shock, and she became convinced that this was his problem. Henderson obtained Adrian's military records and discovered that he had been exposed to horrific scenes of slaughter on the battlefield, including the now notorious Battle of the Somme. He agreed with Sister Thompson's diagnosis and undertook to arrange a transfer for him to a special institution that cared for victims of shell shock.

Before any arrangements could be made a cable arrived from South Africa addressed to Adrian. It was in English and in matter of fact terms informed him that Maria, after a short bout of influenza, had developed pneumonia and had died on July18th, 1916. It was from Johan and did not include any greetings or condolences.

Sister Thompson chose her time carefully. After Adrian had been bathed and made comfortable, she sat at his bedside and took his hand in hers, "Lieutenant, you must please listen to what I have to say. It is most important and however painful it may be to you, you must show me that you understand.

"Your brother has sent a cable from South Africa with some very bad news. Are you listening carefully, lieutenant?"

There was no response, but she continued, "It seems as if your mother contracted pneumonia several weeks ago and after a short illness she passed away peacefully."

Adrian moved his head away. It was the first response he had made since arriving at the hospital. His lips moved slightly and the sister distinctly heard him mumble, "Lieutenant? Lieutenant? My name's not lieutenant." His head sank back on the pillow and his face once again became expressionless.

The following week, in spite of Sister Thompson's disciplined hygiene; she had to cope with a sudden epidemic of influenza among her patients. At first Adrian escaped it, but one morning she found him shivering with a high fever. Henderson diagnosed influenza, complicated by pleurisy.

Simple breathing became a torture and each paroxysm of coughing left him weak and helpless from the pain. The coughing prevented him from sleeping and he was losing weight rapidly.

After a week of this torture, Sister Thompson took Henderson to Adrian's bedside. Pulling back the sheets, she showed the doctor how painfully thin he had become. The lash marks and scars from his wounds gave him a pitiful appearance and, as they watched him, he began to writhe in pain from another coughing fit.

They retreated to the sister's cubicle where she admonished the doctor. "We have to do something about Lieutenant Nel. If he can't get some sleep tonight, he won't make it till morning."

"Do I detect a special interest in this patient, sister? Have those dark good looks and unusual blue eyes influenced you?"

Sister Thompson seethed with anger at the doctor's impertinence but held her tongue.

Henderson realised she was angry and became businesslike, "Very well, sister. We can stop the coughing but then he may drown in his own fluids. But let's try an old-fashioned concoction, I learnt from a wise country doctor in Yorkshire. I will write out the prescription now and you can have the pharmacy prepare it for administration this evening."

The mixture contained whisky, a lot of morphine, some cocaine, lemon juice and sugar. With the help of an assistant, Sister Thompson patiently encouraged Adrian to swallow the complete dose. Within minutes, he became unconscious, his breathing regular but laboured. His coughing disappeared completely. The sister left word with the night nurse to call her if his condition changed.

Adrian remained in a semi-conscious state throughout the next day and slept quietly through the following night. The next morning when he woke he still experienced pain when breathing and had a slight cough but, much to everyone's surprise, sat up in bed and ate his first meal.

Sister Thomson did not rush his recovery. She spoke pleasantly and cheerfully to him each day and showed no reaction to his lack of response. But she was anxious to confirm that he was aware of his mother's death. When she finally broached the subject, he merely nodded his head, obviously having understood from the beginning.

She found his brother's address in Adrian's kit bag and wrote a letter explaining what he had been through and that his future was very uncertain. She asked Johan to be patient as it may take weeks if not months before he recovered sufficiently to write to him. Johan wrote a kind letter of thanks in reply and asked to be informed of any change in Adrian's address. He included a short note in Afrikaans from Hester, full of loving thoughts and encouragement. She also revealed that she and an old school chum, who farmed near Worcester, had become engaged. Her letter went unread but Sister Thompson saved it among his belongings, which included a small worn saddle bag containing a brass telescope.

Although Adrian improved physically every day, he remained completely withdrawn and silent. He could dress and wash himself independently. He ate sparingly, did not read anything and never greeted anyone.

In spite of her exhausting duties, Sister Thompson still found time at the end of each day to chat to him and try to coax a smile from him. The evening before his transfer to a special hospital in Scotland, she sat on the side of his bed and took his hand in hers. She dispensed with his rank, saying, "Adrian, we shall miss you after you leave tomorrow. I hope you will find peace in Scotland for the sake of your brother and sister, who are so worried about you. Look after yourself, dear boy."

She squeezed his hand and much to her amazement, felt his hand take hers firmly in his and hold it for several minutes. Neither said anything but for a few fleeting moments the stress and horrors of the war lifted, as a feeling of profound empathy flowed between them.

Adrian was strong enough to carry his own kit bag onto the train bound for Edinburgh but he refused, gesturing to the medical orderlies to do so. He was still painfully thin and looked like a bony scarecrow on the platform, dressed in baggy convalescent blues. The orderlies were not sympathetic and bundled him into a compartment, warning him to stay put. The train journey to Edinburgh was uneventful apart from the continued animosity between Adrian, an officer, and the orderlies, designated as other ranks. On arrival they were pleased to hand him over to an ambulance attendant, who signed a receipt for the patient and settled him comfortably in the passenger seat.

The drive to the convalescent hospital passed through some attractive countryside and, although Adrian never spoke a word, the driver noticed a change in his demeanour as he watched the landscape unfold. He became noticeably excited as they entered the park-like grounds of the manor house, that had been converted into a temporary hospital for shell-shocked veterans.

A uniformed matron met him at the imposing front door, "Welcome, dear. That's right, come inside and bring your case." She showed no surprise at his refusal to speak. Instead she led him upstairs, allowing him to rest half way. On the second floor they entered a large sitting room that had been converted to a dormitory for six patients. Matron helped him unpack his kit and explained the rules of the house to him, "You will be expected to make your own bed military style each day and to keep your uniform and this corner of the room spick and span. Do you understand, love?"

He showed no signs of understanding as he sat on the edge of his bed, looking over her head at the glorious summer foliage beyond the window.

That night his fellow patients woke him several times, calling out in their sleep, while others moaned and even wept openly. It did not seem to disturb him unduly. He rose early, made his bed carefully and sat quietly on it, waiting for someone to tell him what to do next. Matron soon appeared, "What's this? We haven't bothered to shave or wash before breakfast. Can't have that. Come along now."

She led him to the communal bathroom, made him strip down and take a warm shower. For the first time she noticed his skinny back, scarred by whip lashes and the shrapnel wound. Her heart flooded with sympathy, "Now dry yourself off, dear. Don't you feel much better? I'll leave you to shave on your own; come down to breakfast when you're ready."

When he entered the dining room he had no idea where to sit. He stood pathetically in the doorway; his uniform askew and a perplexed look on his face. One of the patients got up and led him to his table, then helped him order his breakfast from the orderly waiting at table. Local farmers supplied the hospital with fresh eggs and milk, while the bakery in the local village produced excellent bread. After a tentative start, he ate his best meal in months and appeared to enjoy it.

After breakfast he sat on a veranda, sheltered from the wind, and watched a foursome of patients playing croquet on the sunlit lawn. It was a peaceful scene and he was noticeably annoyed when an orderly interrupted his reverie, "Doctor MacIntyre wants to see you, Lieutenant."

He was admitted to a large comfortable study that had formerly housed the manor's library. MacIntyre, the senior consultant, was a broad-shouldered Scot, dressed in the uniform of a major. He moved to the front of his desk to greet Adrian, who disregarded the doctor's outstretched hand.

This did not seem to trouble MacIntyre, who returned behind his desk after settling Adrian in a comfortable chair. "Lieutenant Nel, I have been reading your file for the past half-hour and found it most informative but also very disturbing. You have certainly been exposed to a lot of stress but it is our aim at this establishment to heal the wounds that this dreadful war has left you with."

Adrian did not respond in any way, keeping his gaze fixed on a painting above the mantelpiece.

MacIntyre continued, "I must caution you from the beginning, however, that we can't help you if you don't cooperate. Your recovery will largely depend on your own resolve, with a little help from us. Finally, I want you to realise that if you recover you will not be required to serve again in the army. I'm going to recommend that you be honourably discharged."

The last remark produced a fleeting change in Adrian's expression, but he remained silent. MacIntyre then did his best to elicit a response from him by asking him a series of simple questions, but without success. This did not discourage him as he had treated equally difficult cases of depression in the past. MacIntyre and his partner, Dr. Lucas, had read Jung, Freud and other eminent scholars of human behaviour, but relied mostly on their own practical experience as gifted physicians. They believed that a peaceful and sympathetic environment, without the immediate threat of returning to the front, could slowly restore the mental health of their unfortunate patients, deranged and crushed by the gross inhumanity of war. They used drugs sparingly to relieve pain and to provide restorative sleep, but also relied heavily on volunteer nurses from Edinburgh and the surrounding villages to stimulate interest and some joy in their apathetic patients. MacIntyre gave Adrian a thorough physical examination and recorded the results in his file with the comment that he was not optimistic about his mental recovery.

Adrian's behaviour remained sullen and withdrawn for the next six weeks as high summer turned into early autumn. He slowly recovered his meticulous habits, making his bed perfectly each morning while his uniform and locker were models of neatness. He began to eat more adventurously and started to put on a little weight. He spoke to no one, never smiled and read nothing.

MacIntyre and Lucas were disappointed at his progress and discussed his case frequently. At one of their weekly reviews MacIntyre remarked, "Jim, I'm worried about young Nel. He keeps to the rules and is improving physically, but he's still completely withdrawn and unresponsive. If he continues like this, we shall have to consider transferring him to a civilian hospital. God only knows what will happen to him then."

"Yes," replied Lucas. "The fellow frankly gives me the creeps.

I prefer having to listen to Saunders ranting and raving during one of his attacks to being confronted by Nel's expressionless face. He fixes those startling blue eyes on me and stares right through me. But there's one last thing that we can try."

"What's that, Jim?"

"Do you remember that young volunteer, Megan Lyle? She has a charming personality and has helped several chaps make it through the crisis. Why don't you call her in for a chat and see if she would be willing to help?"

"I'll have a chat with her. Right ... next case please."

Adrian was aware of Megan's presence at the hospital. He had watched her wheeling patients around the garden, playing croquet on the lawn and reading to a blinded veteran. Her neat figure, stylish clothes and long fair hair attracted everyone's attention but it was her exuberant good spirits that had secretly affected him. When the matron told him that Megan would be taking him for a walk the next day, he smiled openly.

Although already late autumn, the next day was sunny and mild for their first walk. He allowed the matron to bundle him up and set off with purpose in his step as she linked her arm in his and gestured towards the direction they should take. MacIntyre was watching from his study window and was touched by the scene.

For the next two weeks, apart from Sundays, they met every morning and regardless of the weather took a long walk together, returning to the hospital for tea and drop scones in front of the fire. Here, they enjoyed the warmth of the elegant common room and the companionship of some of his brother officers.

Each day Adrian showed marked improvement; he began to talk, hesitantly at first, then slowly but fluently. He smiled occasionally at his brother officers and started to page through the newspapers, but without reading them. Every morning he sat near the front door, waiting for Megan's arrival, togged out in his old army greatcoat and his artillery cap minus its insignia. On Sundays his disappointment was obvious and he wandered around aimlessly all day.

During the fourth week after Megan had started seeing him, he experienced something that brought about a pivotal change in his recovery. She arrived one morning lugging what appeared to be a heavy suitcase, "Guess what I have here." She teased Adrian. "No, it's not a sewing machine, nor is it my new hatbox." When she finally opened it up, he saw that it was a gramophone. She cranked it up and fitted a new needle before playing a popular aria sung by Caruso. The music seemed to fill the room. Adrian was transfixed, reached for her hand and held it openly.

From then on his recovery was uneventful, he began to read again and went painfully through Johan and Hester's letters, accepting the tragic loss of his mother. He composed a long letter to Johan and asked Megan's advice about its suitability. She, in turn, felt drawn to her enigmatic charge and felt a tremendous sense of accomplishment for her part in his recovery.

During this time she met regularly with MacIntyre to report on Adrian's progress. "Doctor, you won't believe how much better he is since we started listening to music. He's far more confident, speaks quite articulately now and, best of all, has shown a strong interest in returning to his medical studies." MacIntyre was most interested in the important role that music had played in Adrian's recovery and questioned her closely on that subject.

Another month of long walks, nutritious food, as well as the regular enjoyment of music and good reading, completed his recovery. MacIntyre began to hint at his discharge. He called him to his office one morning and welcomed him warmly, "Good morning, lieutenant. Please sit down and don't look so concerned. I only have good news for you."

"This is not my concerned expression, major. I save that for professors and bank managers."

"Well, talking about professors may be a good starting point for our conversation. As you know, your discharge came through last month and since then Dr. Lucas and I have been negotiating with the War Office to arrange a loan for you to complete your medical studies. Their approval arrived yesterday ..."

Adrian sprang up and interrupted MacIntyre, wringing his hand and slapping his shoulder, "You must be joking!" He exclaimed. "That's absolutely wonderful."

"I thought you would be pleased and you will also be glad to learn that I have spoken to the Dean of Medicine and he assures me that you will be allowed to rejoin the third year class after the Christmas holidays."

Adrian rocked back and forth on his chair with excitement, "I must tell Megan, she'll be just as pleased."

"Indeed," MacIntyre murmured as his voice took on a more serious tone. "Lieutenant, there is, however, one last exercise that you and I must complete before you leave."

"What's that, sir?"

"This may be painful for you but I want you, when you are ready, to come to me and carefully relate in detail your worst experiences at the front. I also want to give you a final physical examination."

Adrian at first looked somewhat crestfallen, but soon pulled himself together and asked, "Why not right now? That is, if you have the time now."

MacIntyre rose from behind his desk and invited him to join him at the fireside where two easy chairs were arranged. After a hesitant start he confided his worst experiences, nightmares and fears to MacIntyre in detail. At the end of this catharsis he was emotionally exhausted, gladly accepted a strong pre-lunch whisky from the doctor and retired to his room where he slept deeply all afternoon.

The next day Megan, decked out in a stylish tweed overcoat, called for Adrian to take him on his usual walk. Her eyes shone with pleasure when he told her the good news.

But this time it was he who took her arm, to guide her through the gate of the manor gardens and a grove of leafless trees rimed with hoarfrost, silent under a leaden Scottish sky.

꒰ ꒱

Credits

The description of Sennacherib fighting the Elamites in 691 BC was adapted from, J. Keegan (1994) *A History of Warfare,* Vintage, New York.

The image on the front cover was adapted from, D. Reitz (1990) *Commando, A Boer Journal of the Boer War,* Jonathan Ball, Johannesburg.

For the factual descriptions of the battles of Colenso and the Somme, much credit is due to D. Saul (1997) *Military Blunders,* Robinson, London.